The Giant Book of Witty Facts

by
Jake Jacobs

* * * * *

Published by Jake Jacobs

The Giant Book of Witty Facts
Copyright© 2023 by Jake Jacobs

1.

Universal Studios is one of the oldest and most iconic film studios in Hollywood, California.

2.

It was founded on April 30, 1912, by Carl Laemmle, a German immigrant.

3.

The studio originally operated under the name Universal Film Manufacturing Company.

4.

Universal Studios is known for its production of classic horror films, including Dracula, Frankenstein, and The Mummy.

5.

In 1915, Universal Studios released the silent film "The Birth of a Nation," which became one of the most controversial and influential films in American history.

6.

Universal Studios introduced the concept of a "studio tour" in 1964, allowing visitors to go behind the scenes and explore the sets and attractions.

7.

The iconic Universal Studios logo features a rotating globe with the words "Universal Pictures" surrounding it.

8.

Universal Studios has produced many successful film franchises, including Jaws, Jurassic Park, and the Fast & Furious series.

9.

In 1968, Universal Studios introduced the world's first "live-action stunt show" called "Fearless Fosdick's Stunt Spectacular."

10.

The studio is home to the famous Universal Studios Hollywood theme park, which opened in 1964.

11.

Universal Studios expanded its theme park business by opening Universal Orlando Resort in 1990.

12.

The Universal Studios theme parks are known for their thrilling rides, immersive experiences, and attractions based on popular movies and TV shows.

13.

In 1999, Universal Studios released the highly successful film "The Blair Witch Project," which became one of the most profitable movies ever made.

14.

Universal Studios is a major player in the animation industry, producing beloved animated films such as Despicable Me, Shrek, and The Secret Life of Pets.

15.

The studio has won numerous Academy Awards for its films, including Best Picture for "Schindler's List" and "American Beauty."

16.

Universal Studios expanded its reach in the entertainment industry by launching the Universal Music Group, one of the world's largest music labels.

17.

The studio has also ventured into television production, creating popular shows such as "The Office," "Parks and Recreation," and "Law & Order: Special Victims Unit."

18.

In 2000, Universal Studios established Focus Features, a specialty film division known for producing critically acclaimed movies.

19.

Universal Studios has a rich history of collaborating with renowned filmmakers, including Steven Spielberg, Alfred Hitchcock, and Ron Howard.

20.

The studio faced financial difficulties in the late 1990s but experienced a revival with the success of franchises like Harry Potter and The Fast and the Furious.

21.

Universal Studios has a significant presence in the international market, with distribution and production operations in countries such as China, India, and the United Kingdom.

22.

The studio has made significant technological advancements, including the introduction of IMAX and 3D films.

23.

Universal Studios launched its own streaming service, Peacock, in 2020, offering a wide range of movies, TV shows, and original content.

24.

The Universal Studios backlot, located in Universal City, California, is one of the largest and most famous working studio lots in the world.

25.

Many iconic film sets and attractions can be found on the Universal Studios backlot, including the famous Bates Motel from the movie "Psycho."

26.

Universal Studios has had its fair share of disasters, including a major fire in 2008 that destroyed several historic sets and archives.

27.

The studio has a long-standing partnership with the toy company Hasbro, resulting in movies based on popular franchises like Transformers and G.I. Joe.

28.

Universal Studios established the Universal Pictures Home Entertainment division to distribute its films for home viewing.

29.

The studio has a reputation for its immersive theme park experiences, with attractions like The Wizarding World of Harry Potter and The Simpsons Ride.

30.

Universal Studios has undergone several ownership changes throughout its history, including mergers with companies like NBC and Comcast.

31.

The studio has a dedicated team of researchers and archivists who work to preserve and restore its extensive film library.

32.

Universal Studios has made significant contributions to the advancement of visual effects technology in the film industry.

33.

The studio has a famous water tank known as the "Wisteria Tank," used for filming water-based scenes in movies like "Jaws."

34.

Universal Studios has a successful partnership with Illumination Entertainment, producing hit animated films like "Minions" and "Sing."

35.

The studio has embraced diversity and inclusivity in its films, promoting representation and tackling social issues through storytelling.

36.

Universal Studios has its own iconic characters, such as the mischievous Minions, who have become pop culture icons.

37.

The studio has collaborated with renowned theme park designers to create immersive experiences, including Universal's Islands of Adventure and Volcano Bay.

38.

Universal Studios has expanded its reach beyond Hollywood and Orlando, with theme parks in Japan and Singapore.

39.

The studio's film franchises have led to the creation of successful merchandise lines, including toys, clothing, and collectibles.

40.

Universal Studios has been recognized with numerous honors and accolades, including a star on the Hollywood Walk of Fame.

41.

The studio actively supports environmental initiatives and sustainable practices within its operations.

42.

Universal Studios has a long-standing commitment to philanthropy and charitable causes, supporting organizations such as the United Way and Red Cross.

43.

The studio has played a significant role in preserving film history through its restoration projects and collaborations with film archives.

44.

Universal Studios has a dedicated fanbase that eagerly anticipates new movie releases and visits its theme parks worldwide.

45.

The studio has faced controversies and criticism over the years, including issues related to representation and creative decision-making.

46.

Universal Studios has utilized innovative marketing strategies, including interactive social media campaigns and viral marketing techniques.

47.

The studio has been at the forefront of digital distribution, exploring new ways to reach audiences through streaming platforms and online content.

48.

Universal Studios has partnered with major retailers to create themed merchandise sections, bringing the magic of its movies to stores worldwide.

49.

The studio actively seeks new talent and fosters the development of emerging filmmakers through initiatives like the Universal Writers Program and the Emerging Directors Program.

50.

Universal Studios continues to shape the entertainment industry through its innovative storytelling, technological advancements, and commitment to delivering memorable experiences for audiences around the world.

51.

Sonos was founded in 2002 by John MacFarlane, Tom Cullen, Trung Mai, and Craig Shelburne.

52.

The company's initial goal was to revolutionize the way people listen to music in their homes by creating a wireless multi-room audio system.

53.

Sonos released its first product, the ZP100, in 2005. It allowed users to wirelessly stream music from their computers to any room in their homes.

54.

Sonos quickly gained popularity and recognition for its innovative approach to home audio systems.

55.

In 2009, Sonos introduced the ZonePlayer S5, a wireless speaker system that integrated amplification, speakers, and streaming capabilities into a single unit.

56.

Sonos expanded its product line over the years, offering a range of speakers, soundbars, and subwoofers, all designed to work seamlessly together in a multi-room setup.

57.

The company's focus on high-quality sound and user-friendly interface has earned it a loyal customer base.

58.

Sonos developed its own wireless technology called SonosNet, which creates a dedicated wireless network for its speakers, ensuring reliable and uninterrupted audio streaming.

59.

In 2011, Sonos launched the Sonos Controller app, which allowed users to control their Sonos systems from their smartphones or tablets.

60.

Sonos has collaborated with various music streaming services, including Spotify, Apple Music, and Amazon Music, to offer seamless integration and access to millions of songs.

61.

Sonos products are known for their sleek and minimalist design, allowing them to blend seamlessly into any home decor.

62.

The company has received numerous awards for its products' design, innovation, and sound quality.

63.

Sonos has been at the forefront of voice-controlled smart speakers, integrating Amazon Alexa and later Google Assistant into some of its products.

64.

Sonos introduced Trueplay, a technology that automatically tunes the sound of its speakers to adapt to the acoustics of any room.

65.

In 2018, Sonos went public and became a publicly traded company on the Nasdaq Stock Market.

66.

Sonos has a strong commitment to sustainability, striving to minimize its environmental impact through initiatives like using recycled and recyclable materials in its products.

67.

The company has implemented energy-saving features in its products, such as auto-sleep and power management capabilities.

68.

Sonos has a robust customer support system, offering online resources, live chat, and phone support to assist users with any technical or setup issues.

69.

Sonos has a strong community of users and enthusiasts who actively share their experiences, tips, and recommendations on online forums and social media.

70.

Sonos has expanded its product offerings to include home theater systems, outdoor speakers, and architectural speakers for professional installations.

71.

The company has partnered with renowned designers and brands, such as IKEA, to create unique and integrated home audio solutions.

72.

Sonos has embraced open platform integration, allowing users to control their Sonos systems through third-party apps and voice assistants.

73.

The company continuously updates its software to add new features, improve performance, and enhance the overall user experience.

74.

Sonos has a global presence, with products sold in over 100 countries and support for multiple languages.

75.

Sonos has received widespread critical acclaim for its products, earning accolades from technology publications and industry experts.

76.

The company has a strong commitment to privacy and data security, ensuring that customer information is protected.

77.

Sonos has actively engaged in philanthropic initiatives, including supporting music education programs and providing audio equipment to schools and community centers.

78.

The Sonos Sound Experience Center in New York City showcases the capabilities of Sonos products through immersive and interactive installations.

79.

Sonos has collaborated with artists, musicians, and filmmakers to create unique audio experiences and exclusive content.

80.

The company has a dedicated research and development team, constantly exploring new technologies and innovations in audio.

81.

Sonos has a customer loyalty program called Sonos Sound System, offering exclusive benefits and rewards to its most loyal customers.

82.

The company has a strong focus on customer feedback and uses it to drive product improvements and enhancements.

83.

Sonos offers regular software updates to ensure compatibility with new devices and technologies.

84.

Sonos products are known for their durability and longevity, with many customers using them for years without experiencing significant issues.

85.

Sonos has established strategic partnerships with home automation companies, allowing users to integrate their Sonos systems into larger smart home ecosystems.

86.

The company has a dedicated team of audio engineers and acoustics experts who work to optimize the sound quality of its products.

87.

Sonos has a transparent and customer-centric warranty and return policy, ensuring customer satisfaction and peace of mind.

88.

The company actively engages with its user community, seeking feedback and ideas for new product features and improvements.

89.

Sonos has expanded its presence in the commercial market, providing audio solutions for businesses, restaurants, and hospitality venues.

90.

The company has received numerous industry accolades and awards for its products' performance and innovation.

91.

Sonos has a strong commitment to diversity and inclusion, promoting a diverse workforce and fostering an inclusive company culture.

92.

The company actively supports music and cultural events, sponsoring concerts, festivals, and industry conferences.

93.

Sonos has a comprehensive environmental sustainability program, focusing on reducing its carbon footprint, waste reduction, and responsible sourcing.

94.

The company has established partnerships with music artists and labels, offering exclusive content and experiences to Sonos users.

95.

Sonos has a dedicated team of customer experience professionals who provide personalized support and assistance to users.

96.

The company has an active social media presence, engaging with its community through platforms like Instagram, Twitter, and Facebook.

97.

Sonos has a strong commitment to product compatibility and interoperability, ensuring that its products work seamlessly with a wide range of devices and platforms.

98.

The company actively collaborates with other audio brands and technology companies to create integrated and connected audio solutions.

99.

Sonos has a user-friendly setup process, with guided instructions and intuitive interfaces to help users get their systems up and running quickly.

100.

The company is continually exploring new opportunities and partnerships to expand its product offerings and deliver innovative audio solutions to customers worldwide.

101.

The Prudence Crandall House, located in Canterbury, Connecticut, is a historic site associated with the abolitionist movement and women's rights.

102.

The house was built in 1808 and served as the residence of Prudence Crandall, an educator and activist.

103.

Prudence Crandall is known for her groundbreaking work in establishing a school for African American girls during a time of racial segregation in the United States.

104.

In 1833, Prudence Crandall converted her private school for young women into the Canterbury Female Boarding School, which admitted African American students.

105.

The decision to admit African American students faced strong opposition from the local community, including threats and acts of violence.

106.

Prudence Crandall persisted in her mission to provide education to African American girls, despite facing significant resistance and legal challenges.

107.

The Canterbury Female Boarding School attracted students from various states, including New York, Massachusetts, and Rhode Island.

108.

The school faced ongoing harassment, including vandalism, boycotting, and the poisoning of the school's well.

109.

Prudence Crandall and her students faced social isolation and hostility from the local community.

110.

In 1834, the Connecticut General Assembly passed the "Black Law," which made it illegal to educate African American students from out of state.

111.

Prudence Crandall was arrested and charged with violating the "Black Law." She faced trial and was convicted, but the verdict was later overturned.

112.

The Connecticut General Assembly then passed the "Black Law II," which made it illegal to operate an integrated school.

113.

Facing mounting pressure and legal obstacles, Prudence Crandall was forced to close the Canterbury Female Boarding School in 1834.

114.

The closure of the school marked a significant setback for the education of African American girls in the United States.

115.

Prudence Crandall continued her activism and advocacy for women's rights and abolition even after the school's closure.

116.

The Prudence Crandall House is now a designated National Historic Landmark and is listed on the National Register of Historic Places.

117.

The house has been restored to reflect its appearance during Prudence Crandall's residency and operates as a museum and educational center.

118.

The museum features exhibits on Prudence Crandall's life, the history of the Canterbury Female Boarding School, and the fight for racial equality.

119.

Visitors to the Prudence Crandall House can explore the various rooms, including the classroom, bedroom, and parlor, and learn about the daily life of the school.

120.

The site offers guided tours and educational programs that highlight the significance of Prudence Crandall's work and its impact on American history.

121.

The Prudence Crandall House serves as a reminder of the struggles and sacrifices made by early advocates of racial and gender equality.

122.

The house is a symbol of resistance against discrimination and a testament to the courage and determination of Prudence Crandall and her students.

123.

Prudence Crandall's fight for educational equality is considered a precursor to the civil rights movement and a milestone in the history of African American education.

124.

The Prudence Crandall House is part of the Connecticut Freedom Trail, a collection of historic sites related to African American history and the abolitionist movement in the state.

125.

The site offers educational resources and materials for teachers and students, fostering an understanding of the importance of equality and social justice.

126.

The Prudence Crandall House has been recognized for its historical significance by numerous organizations and institutions, including the National Trust for Historic Preservation.

127.

The house stands as a physical representation of the struggles and triumphs of the abolitionist movement in Connecticut.

128.

Prudence Crandall's dedication to education and equality inspired subsequent generations of activists and reformers.

129.

The Prudence Crandall House serves as a reminder of the power of education in challenging societal norms and promoting social change.

130.

The site hosts special events and programs throughout the year, including lectures, workshops, and exhibitions that explore various aspects of Prudence Crandall's life and legacy.

131.

The Prudence Crandall House continues to be a gathering place for individuals and groups interested in civil rights, social justice, and educational equity.

132.

The house and its surrounding grounds provide a tranquil and picturesque setting for reflection and contemplation.

133.

The Prudence Crandall House is an important landmark in the history of women's education, highlighting the challenges and triumphs of women educators in the early 19th century.

134.

Prudence Crandall's story is a testament to the resilience and determination of individuals who strive for justice and equality.

135.

The Prudence Crandall House stands as a symbol of the ongoing struggle for equal access to education for all individuals, regardless of race or gender.

136.

The museum offers educational programs for school groups, engaging students in discussions about civil rights, tolerance, and equality.

137.

The Prudence Crandall House attracts visitors from around the country and serves as an educational resource for scholars, researchers, and history enthusiasts.

138.

The site has been featured in various publications and media outlets, drawing attention to Prudence Crandall's important role in American history.

139.

The Prudence Crandall House is a place of pilgrimage for those interested in the fight for civil rights and the stories of unsung heroes.

140.

The house stands as a testament to the importance of preserving and sharing the stories of marginalized individuals who have made significant contributions to society.

141.

The Prudence Crandall House is a valuable resource for understanding the challenges faced by women and minorities in the pursuit of education and equal rights.

142.

The museum offers interpretive exhibits that explore the broader historical context of Prudence Crandall's work, including the abolitionist movement and the struggle for women's rights.

143.

The Prudence Crandall House serves as a catalyst for dialogue and reflection on the ongoing quest for social justice and equality.

144.

The museum collaborates with local schools, universities, and community organizations to promote awareness and understanding of Prudence Crandall's legacy.

145.

The Prudence Crandall House has become a focal point for community engagement, hosting events that celebrate diversity, inclusivity, and the power of education.

146.

The site provides a platform for contemporary voices and perspectives, offering exhibits and programs that explore the continued relevance of Prudence Crandall's story.

147.

The Prudence Crandall House represents a significant chapter in the history of the struggle for civil rights in the United States.

148.

The museum encourages visitors to consider their own roles in creating a more inclusive and equitable society.

149.

The Prudence Crandall House is an essential destination for anyone interested in the stories of those who challenged social norms and fought for equality.

150.

The site stands as a reminder of the transformative power of individuals who dare to challenge injustice and inspire change.

151.

The James Dwight Dana House is a historic residence located in New Haven, Connecticut.

152.

The house was designed by renowned architect Henry Austin in the High Victorian Gothic style.

153.

It was built in 1850 and served as the home of James Dwight Dana, a prominent American geologist and mineralogist.

154.

James Dwight Dana is best known for his extensive scientific research and publications on geology, mineralogy, and volcanology.

155.

The house is named in honor of James Dwight Dana and stands as a testament to his significant contributions to the field of earth sciences.

156.

The James Dwight Dana House is listed on the National Register of Historic Places and is a designated National Historic Landmark.

157.

The house features a unique architectural design characterized by pointed arches, intricate tracery, and decorative details inspired by medieval Gothic aesthetics.

158.

The interior of the house is adorned with beautiful woodwork, stained glass windows, and ornate plasterwork.

159.

The James Dwight Dana House is a well-preserved example of Victorian-era domestic architecture in New England.

160.

The house served as the residence of James Dwight Dana until his death in 1895.

161.

After Dana's passing, the house remained in the family and was occupied by his descendants for several generations.

162.

In 1974, the James Dwight Dana House was acquired by Yale University and became part of the Yale campus.

163.

The house is located near the renowned Yale School of Forestry and Environmental Studies, emphasizing its connection to the field of earth sciences.

164.

Today, the James Dwight Dana House serves as a faculty residence for the Yale School of Forestry and Environmental Studies.

165.

The house is occasionally used for academic and social events, providing a unique and historic setting for gatherings and celebrations.

166.

The architecture of the James Dwight Dana House reflects the 19th-century fascination with the Gothic Revival style, which sought to evoke a sense of romanticism and medieval grandeur.

167.

The exterior of the house features a steeply pitched roof, pointed gables, and elaborate decorative elements.

168.

The house is constructed of brick, with carefully crafted details that showcase the craftsmanship and attention to detail prevalent during the Victorian era.

169.

Inside the house, visitors can admire the grand staircase, intricate woodwork, and beautiful period furnishings.

170.

The James Dwight Dana House is surrounded by well-maintained gardens, adding to its picturesque charm.

171.

The house's location in New Haven, Connecticut, places it in close proximity to other notable Yale University buildings and attractions.

172.

The James Dwight Dana House stands as a reminder of the rich intellectual history and scientific legacy of Yale University.

173.

James Dwight Dana was a respected professor at Yale and held the position of the university's first professor of geology.

174.

Throughout his career, Dana made significant contributions to the study of minerals, volcanoes, and the geological history of North America.

175.

Dana's research and publications played a crucial role in advancing the field of geology and establishing a scientific understanding of the Earth's processes.

176.

The James Dwight Dana House serves as a memorial to the achievements and intellectual pursuits of its namesake.

177.

The house's historical significance extends beyond its association with James Dwight Dana, as it represents the architectural trends and cultural values of the Victorian era.

178.

Visitors to the James Dwight Dana House can gain insights into the personal and professional life of James Dwight Dana through guided tours and interpretive exhibits.

179.

The house offers a glimpse into the daily routines and domestic lives of prominent 19th-century intellectuals and their families.

180.

The James Dwight Dana House showcases the importance of scientific inquiry and intellectual pursuits in shaping society and driving progress.

181.

The preservation of the house allows future generations to appreciate and learn from the accomplishments of James Dwight Dana and the historical context in which he lived.

182.

The house's location within the Yale campus ensures that it remains an integral part of the university's academic and cultural landscape.

183.

The James Dwight Dana House stands as a symbol of Yale's commitment to fostering a rich intellectual environment and advancing scientific knowledge.

184.

The house provides an immersive experience of stepping back in time, allowing visitors to explore the intersection of science, architecture, and history.

185.

The James Dwight Dana House is often included in architectural tours of New Haven, showcasing the city's diverse architectural heritage.

186.

The house's inclusion on the National Register of Historic Places highlights its architectural and historical significance on a national level.

187.

The James Dwight Dana House contributes to the overall aesthetic and character of the Yale University campus, blending harmoniously with other historic and modern buildings.

188.

The house's proximity to other scientific and academic institutions within Yale fosters interdisciplinary collaboration and intellectual exchange.

189.

The preservation and maintenance of the James Dwight Dana House are overseen by Yale University, ensuring its long-term protection and accessibility.

190.

The house serves as a source of inspiration and admiration for those interested in the fields of geology, earth sciences, and architectural history.

191.

The James Dwight Dana House has been recognized for its architectural merit and historical importance by architectural and preservation organizations.

192.

The house's architectural features, such as its pointed arches and intricate woodwork, exemplify the craftsmanship and attention to detail of the Victorian era.

193.

The James Dwight Dana House embodies the values of education, scientific inquiry, and intellectual curiosity that have been central to Yale University's mission since its founding.

194.

The house's significance extends beyond its physical structure, as it serves as a place of contemplation and reflection on the contributions of James Dwight Dana and the broader scientific community.

195.

The James Dwight Dana House is an integral part of Yale's efforts to preserve and showcase its rich heritage and to engage the public in the exploration of knowledge and ideas.

196.

The house provides a link between past and present, connecting visitors to the legacy of scientific exploration and discovery that continues to shape our understanding of the world.

197.

The James Dwight Dana House offers an opportunity to explore the intersection of science and culture, showcasing how scientific advancements can influence art, architecture, and society.

198.

The house's historical and cultural significance extends beyond Yale University, as it contributes to the broader narrative of scientific progress and intellectual pursuits.

199.

The preservation of the James Dwight Dana House is a testament to the value society places on preserving our scientific and intellectual heritage.

200.

The James Dwight Dana House serves as a reminder of the lasting impact of individuals who dedicate their lives to the pursuit of knowledge and the advancement of human understanding.

201.

The Great Grey Owl, also known as the Lapland Owl or Phantom of the North, is one of the largest species of owls in the world.

202.

It has a wingspan of up to 1.3 meters (4.3 feet) and can weigh between 580 to 1,900 grams (1.3 to 4.2 pounds).

203.

The Great Grey Owl is native to the northern regions of North America, Europe, and Asia, inhabiting forests and taiga habitats.

204.

It is recognized for its striking appearance, with a large rounded head, piercing yellow eyes, and a facial disc that enhances its hearing capabilities.

205.

The owl's plumage is predominantly grey, with intricate patterns of dark bars and streaks that provide excellent camouflage among tree trunks and branches.

206.

The Great Grey Owl is primarily a nocturnal hunter, relying on its exceptional hearing to locate prey, such as small mammals like voles and mice.

207.

Unlike many other owl species, the Great Grey Owl has a low-pitched and soft hooting call that carries over long distances.

208.

These owls have specialized feathers on their wings that allow for silent flight, enabling them to approach prey undetected.

209.

Great Grey Owls have excellent vision, with forward-facing eyes that provide a wide field of view, allowing them to accurately locate and target prey.

210.

They have remarkable hearing, with asymmetrically positioned ears that help them pinpoint the exact location of prey by detecting subtle differences in sound intensity and arrival time.

211.

The Great Grey Owl is known for its unique hunting technique called "still-hunting," where it perches and waits patiently for prey to move before making a swift and silent attack.

212.

These owls are not migratory and tend to establish territories that can range from 25 to 400 hectares (62 to 988 acres).

213.

Great Grey Owls are monogamous and typically mate for life, with pairs staying together throughout the year.

214.

The female owl lays a clutch of 3 to 5 eggs, which are incubated by both parents for about 28 to 36 days.

215.

The young owls, known as owlets, hatch covered in white down feathers and are dependent on their parents for food and protection.

216.

The owlets remain in the nest for around 4 to 5 weeks, after which they begin to explore the surrounding area and learn to fly.

217.

The Great Grey Owl has an impressive lifespan, with some individuals living up to 13 years in the wild.

218.

These owls have faced habitat loss due to logging activities and changes in forest management practices, leading to population declines in some regions.

219.

Conservation efforts have been implemented to protect the habitat and breeding sites of the Great Grey Owl, ensuring their long-term survival.

220.

In some Native American cultures, the Great Grey Owl is considered a symbol of wisdom and is associated with mystical and spiritual beliefs.

221.

The Great Grey Owl is a popular subject for birdwatchers and wildlife photographers due to its unique appearance and elusive nature.

222.

It has been featured in various forms of art, literature, and folklore, often depicted as a wise and mysterious creature.

223.

The Great Grey Owl is an indicator species, meaning its presence or absence in an ecosystem can reflect the overall health of the environment.

224.

Due to their large size and distinctive features, Great Grey Owls are easily recognizable and are sometimes referred to as the "ghost of the north."

225.

These owls have an exceptional ability to locate prey under thick snow cover by using their keen hearing to detect movement.

226.

Great Grey Owls are adapted to withstand cold temperatures, with feathers that provide excellent insulation and protect them from harsh winter conditions.

227.

The owls have specialized facial feathers that help direct sound to their ears, enhancing their ability to locate prey even in dense vegetation.

228.

Great Grey Owls are known to defend their nests vigorously, using their sharp talons and powerful wings to ward off potential threats.

229.

The owls are known to have excellent parenting skills, with both male and female participating in feeding and caring for their young.

230.

In the wild, Great Grey Owls are solitary birds and prefer to maintain a wide territory, often avoiding contact with other individuals.

231.

The Great Grey Owl's diet primarily consists of small mammals, but it can also prey on birds, insects, and occasionally fish.

232.

They have a specialized hunting strategy known as "sit-and-wait," where they perch on high vantage points and scan the surroundings for potential prey.

233.

The Great Grey Owl has large facial discs that help direct sound waves into its ears, enhancing its ability to locate prey in complete darkness.

234.

These owls have long wings and a buoyant flight style, which allows them to glide silently through the forest while searching for prey.

235.

The Great Grey Owl is an apex predator in its ecosystem and plays a vital role in maintaining a balanced population of prey species.

236.

They are known for their aggressive territorial behavior and will defend their nesting sites from intruders, including other owls and predators.

237.

Great Grey Owls have excellent camouflage abilities, with their grey plumage blending seamlessly with the tree bark and foliage.

238.

They have sharp talons and a powerful grip that enables them to catch and secure their prey quickly and efficiently.

239.

Great Grey Owls are non-migratory birds and generally stay within their home range throughout the year.

240.

The owls have a unique ability to turn their heads up to 270 degrees, allowing them to scan their surroundings without moving their bodies.

241.

Great Grey Owls have specialized feathers on their legs and feet, which protect them from extreme temperatures and enable them to walk on snow without sinking.

242.

These owls have a varied repertoire of vocalizations, including hoots, growls, hisses, and clucks, which they use for communication and territorial defense.

243.

Great Grey Owls have incredible eyesight, with large yellow eyes that are adapted for low light conditions, allowing them to see in dimly lit environments.

244.

They have a complex digestive system that allows them to regurgitate undigested material, such as bones and fur, in the form of pellets.

245.

The Great Grey Owl has a specialized wing structure that enables it to fly silently, making it a stealthy predator.

246.

These owls are known for their exceptional flying skills, with the ability to maneuver through dense forests and navigate narrow spaces with ease.

247.

Great Grey Owls are known to build their nests in tree cavities, abandoned nests of other large birds, or on the ground in dense vegetation.

248.

They have an acute sense of hearing, which allows them to locate prey even when it is hidden under thick foliage or snow cover.

249.

Great Grey Owls have a slow and deliberate flight pattern, allowing them to maintain control and accuracy when hunting.

250.

These magnificent owls are an important symbol of the wilderness and are highly regarded for their beauty, grace, and unique adaptations.

251.

The Great White African Pelican, also known as the Eastern White Pelican, is one of the largest species of pelicans in the world.

252.

It is native to parts of Africa, including the eastern and southern regions, and is found in various aquatic habitats such as lakes, rivers, and coastal areas.

253.

The Great White African Pelican has a wingspan that can reach up to 3.5 meters (11.5 feet), making it one of the largest flying birds.

254.

It has a distinct white plumage with black wingtips and a yellowish or pinkish bill, which develops a prominent throat pouch during breeding season.

255.

These pelicans are highly social birds and often form large flocks, especially during feeding and nesting periods.

256.

Great White African Pelicans are known for their spectacular group fishing behavior, where they work together to encircle fish and scoop them up in their bills.

257.

They have a specialized throat pouch that can expand to accommodate large amounts of fish and water, allowing them to store and transport food.

258.

Great White African Pelicans are primarily piscivorous, feeding on fish as their main source of diet. They are capable of consuming several kilograms of fish in a single feeding session.

259.

Despite their large size, these pelicans are agile swimmers and divers, using their webbed feet and powerful wings to propel themselves underwater.

260.

During the breeding season, male Great White African Pelicans develop vivid pinkish or orange-colored facial skin and a crest on their heads.

261.

They engage in elaborate courtship displays, including head-swaying, bill-clapping, and wing-flapping, to attract a mate.

262.

Nesting colonies of Great White African Pelicans are usually established on small islands or secluded areas near water bodies, providing protection from predators.

263.

Both males and females participate in nest-building, constructing large, shallow nests made of sticks, reeds, and vegetation.

264.

Female pelicans typically lay 1 to 3 eggs, which are incubated by both parents for about 30 to 35 days.

265.

The chicks are born naked and helpless but quickly grow a downy feather coat. They are dependent on their parents for food and protection.

266.

Great White African Pelicans have a long lifespan, with individuals living up to 25 years in the wild and even longer in captivity.

267.

These pelicans are highly adaptable and can be found in a variety of habitats, including freshwater lakes, coastal lagoons, estuaries, and even inland wetlands.

268.

They are known for their graceful flight, soaring high in the sky on thermals and using their large wings to cover great distances during migration.

269.

Great White African Pelicans undertake seasonal migrations, moving between breeding and non-breeding areas in search of suitable feeding grounds.

270.

They have been observed flying long distances in a V-formation, which helps reduce wind resistance and allows them to conserve energy during flight.

271.

The Great White African Pelican has a complex vocal repertoire, including various grunts, hisses, and bill-clattering sounds used for communication within the colony.

272.

These pelicans are highly skilled at using their large bills to catch and manipulate slippery fish, using their tongues to guide prey into their pouches.

273.

Great White African Pelicans have been known to engage in kleptoparasitism, stealing fish from other birds such as cormorants and gulls.

274.

They have excellent eyesight, allowing them to spot fish from above while soaring in the air or floating on the water's surface.

275.

Great White African Pelicans have a unique adaptation called the gular flutter, which involves rapid vibrations of their throat pouch to cool themselves in hot weather.

276.

They are capable of drinking saltwater and have specialized salt glands near their eyes that help them excrete excess salt from their bodies.

277.

These pelicans are highly gregarious and often interact with other bird species, such as herons, ibises, and storks, during feeding and roosting.

278.

Great White African Pelicans play an important ecological role in their habitats, as their feeding behavior helps regulate fish populations.

279.

They are also considered an indicator species, reflecting the health of aquatic ecosystems and the availability of food resources.

280.

Great White African Pelicans have been revered in many cultures and are often associated with grace, beauty, and freedom.

281.

They have been depicted in various forms of art, including paintings, sculptures, and literature, symbolizing elegance and tranquility.

282.

These pelicans have faced conservation challenges due to habitat loss, pollution, and human disturbance, leading to population declines in certain areas.

283.

Conservation efforts have been implemented to protect their nesting sites and ensure sustainable fishing practices in their habitats.

284.

Great White African Pelicans have been studied extensively for their behavior, breeding biology, and ecological interactions, providing valuable insights into their conservation needs.

285.

They are listed as a species of least concern on the IUCN Red List, indicating that their population is currently stable.

286.

Great White African Pelicans have been successfully bred in captivity, contributing to conservation and educational programs around the world.

287.

They are popular attractions in many zoos and wildlife parks, where visitors can observe their impressive size, feeding habits, and aerial acrobatics.

288.

Great White African Pelicans have been featured in numerous documentaries and nature films, showcasing their incredible abilities and captivating beauty.

289.

They are protected by national and international laws in many countries, ensuring their conservation and sustainable management.

290.

These pelicans have been the subject of scientific research exploring their feeding behavior, migration patterns, and social dynamics within colonies.

291.

Great White African Pelicans have inspired conservation initiatives and educational campaigns aimed at raising awareness about the importance of wetland habitats and their associated biodiversity.

292.

They are known for their strong parental instincts, with both parents actively participating in feeding and caring for their young.

293.

Great White African Pelicans have been observed engaging in playful behaviors, such as splashing in the water, chasing each other, and performing aerial acrobatics.

294.

They have been known to exhibit courtship rituals even outside of the breeding season, displaying their elaborate plumage and engaging in synchronized swimming patterns.

295.

Great White African Pelicans have been trained in some parts of the world for fishing purposes, where they work alongside fishermen to catch fish in lakes and rivers.

296.

These pelicans are highly adaptable to human-altered environments and can be found near human settlements, including fishing harbors and fish farms.

297.

They have been the focus of local folklore and cultural traditions in many regions, representing symbols of abundance, fertility, and divine protection.

298.

Great White African Pelicans have been successfully reintroduced into areas where their populations were previously extinct or severely depleted.

299.

They are considered flagship species for wetland conservation, serving as ambassadors for the preservation of their unique habitats and associated biodiversity.

300.

Great White African Pelicans are awe-inspiring creatures, captivating both scientists and nature enthusiasts with their size, grace, and remarkable adaptations for aquatic life.

301.

Fidelity Investments was founded in 1946 by Edward C. Johnson II as Fidelity Management & Research Company.

302.

It initially focused on managing mutual funds for individual investors and pioneered the concept of the modern mutual fund.

303.

The company's first mutual fund, the Fidelity Fund, was launched in 1947.

304.

Fidelity became one of the first firms to offer self-service brokerage accounts, allowing investors to trade stocks and bonds online.

305.

In the 1970s, Fidelity introduced the first money market fund, which provided investors with a low-risk, high-liquidity investment option.

306.

Fidelity was an early adopter of technology, introducing computer systems to manage and track investments.

307.

In 1982, Fidelity launched the first online trading platform, giving investors direct access to markets.

308.

Fidelity introduced 401(k) retirement plans in 1981, helping to popularize these tax-advantaged retirement savings accounts.

309.

The company expanded its international presence in the 1990s, opening offices in Europe, Asia, and Latin America.

310.

Fidelity established its retail brokerage arm, Fidelity Brokerage Services, in 1983, providing individual investors with access to a wide range of investment products.

311.

In the late 1990s, Fidelity launched its online brokerage platform, enabling investors to trade stocks and other securities online.

312.

Fidelity has a strong focus on research, employing a large team of analysts and economists to provide insights and recommendations to investors.

313.

The company has a long history of innovation in financial technology, introducing tools and platforms to help investors manage their portfolios more effectively.

314.

Fidelity played a significant role in the growth of the exchange-traded fund (ETF) industry, launching its first ETFs in 2003.

315.

Fidelity offers a wide range of investment products and services, including mutual funds, ETFs, individual retirement accounts (IRAs), annuities, and brokerage accounts.

316.

Fidelity has a strong commitment to customer service, providing investors with access to knowledgeable representatives and online resources.

317.

The company has been recognized for its employee benefits and workplace culture, consistently ranking among the top employers in the financial services industry.

318.

Fidelity has made several acquisitions throughout its history to expand its business and capabilities, including the acquisition of Contrafund in 1967 and the acquisition of several smaller brokerage firms.

319.

Fidelity has been a leader in providing retirement planning and investment guidance, offering tools and resources to help individuals plan for their financial future.

320.

The company has a strong focus on investor education, providing resources and educational materials to help individuals make informed investment decisions.

321.

Fidelity has a robust online platform that allows investors to access their accounts, conduct transactions, and research investment options.

322.

Fidelity has been recognized for its philanthropic efforts, supporting various charitable causes and community initiatives.

323.

The company has a strong commitment to diversity and inclusion, promoting equal opportunities for employees and supporting diverse business partnerships.

324.

Fidelity has received numerous awards and accolades for its financial products, services, and customer satisfaction.

325.

The company has a large and loyal customer base, with millions of individuals and institutions trusting Fidelity with their investments.

326.

Fidelity has weathered various market downturns and economic crises throughout its history, demonstrating resilience and adaptability.

327.

The company has a strong track record of managing assets and generating returns for its clients.

328.

Fidelity has expanded its offerings beyond traditional investment products, venturing into areas such as digital currencies and blockchain technology.

329.

Fidelity has embraced environmental, social, and governance (ESG) investing, providing ESG-focused investment options and integrating sustainability factors into its investment strategies.

330.

The company has a strong commitment to cybersecurity and data protection, implementing robust measures to safeguard investor information.

331.

Fidelity has been at the forefront of technological advancements in the financial industry, exploring applications of artificial intelligence, machine learning, and big data analytics.

332.

The company has a strong corporate governance structure, with a board of directors that provides oversight and strategic guidance.

333.

Fidelity has a global presence, serving clients in over 40 countries around the world.

334.

The company has a strong track record of managing institutional assets, providing investment solutions to pension funds, endowments, and other institutional investors.

335.

Fidelity has been recognized as a trusted and reputable brand in the financial services industry, instilling confidence in investors.

336.

The company has a robust compliance and regulatory framework, ensuring adherence to applicable laws and regulations.

337.

Fidelity has been a proponent of investor empowerment, advocating for shareholder rights and corporate governance reforms.

338.

The company has a long-term investment approach, emphasizing the importance of disciplined investing and long-term wealth creation.

339.

Fidelity has a diverse team of investment professionals with expertise in various asset classes and investment strategies.

340.

The company has been a leader in retirement income planning, providing solutions to help individuals manage their finances in retirement.

341.

Fidelity has been an advocate for financial literacy, promoting the importance of financial education and empowering individuals to make informed financial decisions.

342.

The company has a strong commitment to innovation, continually exploring new technologies and strategies to enhance its offerings.

343.

Fidelity has a robust research and analysis team, providing timely market insights and investment recommendations to clients.

344.

The company has a comprehensive risk management framework, monitoring and mitigating risks associated with its investment activities.

345.

Fidelity has a strong corporate social responsibility program, supporting environmental sustainability, community development, and employee volunteerism.

346.

The company has embraced digital transformation, leveraging technology to enhance its operations, improve customer experiences, and streamline processes.

347.

Fidelity has been recognized for its commitment to corporate ethics and integrity, adhering to high ethical standards in its business practices.

348.

The company has a strong focus on long-term client relationships, providing personalized services and tailored investment solutions.

349.

Fidelity has been a leader in retirement plan services, offering employer-sponsored retirement plans and participant education programs.

350.

The company has a strong financial position, backed by its track record, assets under management, and reputation in the financial services industry.

351.

Patagonia was founded in 1973 by Yvon Chouinard as a small climbing gear company.

352.

The company's original mission was to create high-quality, durable outdoor clothing and gear for climbers and outdoor enthusiasts.

353.

Patagonia takes its name from the region in South America known for its rugged and pristine natural landscapes.

354.

The company's early products included climbing gear such as pitons, carabiners, and clothing made from durable materials.

355.

In the 1980s, Patagonia expanded its product line to include outdoor apparel for various activities, including skiing, hiking, and camping.

356.

Patagonia has been a pioneer in the use of recycled and sustainable materials in its products. It introduced recycled polyester in its fleece jackets in the 1990s.

357.

In 1996, Patagonia became one of the first companies to launch a corporate environmental campaign, called "1% for the Planet," committing to donate 1% of its sales to environmental causes.

358.

Patagonia has been vocal about its commitment to environmental activism and sustainability, advocating for the protection of natural spaces and the reduction of carbon emissions.

359.

The company has actively supported grassroots environmental organizations through its grants program, funding projects that focus on conservation, biodiversity, and climate change.

360.

Patagonia has implemented initiatives to reduce its environmental impact, such as using organic cotton in its clothing, investing in renewable energy, and reducing water usage in its manufacturing processes.

361.

The company has taken a strong stance on social and labor issues, ensuring fair labor practices in its supply chain and advocating for workers' rights.

362.

Patagonia's "Worn Wear" program encourages customers to repair, reuse, and recycle their clothing, reducing waste and extending the life of its products.

363.

Patagonia was one of the first outdoor apparel companies to offer a lifetime warranty on its products, reflecting its commitment to durability and longevity.

364.

In 2011, Patagonia launched its "Footprint Chronicles," an interactive website that provides transparency into its supply chain and manufacturing processes.

365.

The company has made significant efforts to minimize its carbon footprint, including offsetting its emissions, implementing energy-efficient practices, and supporting renewable energy projects.

366.

Patagonia has a strong commitment to fair trade, working with suppliers that adhere to fair labor practices and ensuring safe working conditions.

367.

The company has been involved in various environmental and social justice campaigns, advocating for public lands protection, climate action, and corporate responsibility.

368.

Patagonia has been recognized for its commitment to sustainability and responsible business practices, receiving numerous awards and certifications.

369.

The company has a unique corporate culture that encourages work-life balance, creativity, and a connection to nature. Employees are given flexible work schedules and encouraged to pursue outdoor activities.

370.

Patagonia has a strong focus on employee well-being, offering benefits such as onsite childcare, paid sabbaticals, and volunteer opportunities.

371.

The company's headquarters in Ventura, California, is known for its environmentally friendly design and sustainable features, such as solar panels and water-saving measures.

372.

Patagonia has collaborated with other brands and organizations to promote environmental causes and raise awareness about conservation.

373.

The company has a strong online presence and engages with its customers through social media, sharing stories and initiatives related to its mission.

374.

Patagonia's marketing campaigns often feature inspiring stories of adventurers and environmental activists who embody the brand's values.

375.

The company has been a leader in sustainable business practices, sharing its knowledge and expertise with other companies through conferences and workshops.

376.

Patagonia has established partnerships with environmental organizations and universities to conduct research and develop innovative solutions to environmental challenges.

377.

The company has published books and documentaries that highlight environmental issues and inspire action, such as "The Responsible Company" and "180° South."

378.

Patagonia's commitment to corporate social responsibility has helped shape the industry's approach to sustainability, influencing other companies to adopt similar practices.

379.

The company has faced criticism and controversy at times for its strong stances on political and environmental issues, but it has remained committed to its values.

380.

Patagonia has a strong customer loyalty base, with many individuals identifying with the brand's mission and values.

381.

The company has expanded its retail presence globally, with stores in various countries, including the United States, Europe, and Japan.

382.

Patagonia has diversified its product offerings to include accessories, footwear, and lifestyle products while maintaining a focus on sustainability and quality.

383.

The company has supported environmental education programs and initiatives, aiming to inspire the next generation of environmental stewards.

384.

Patagonia's commitment to transparency extends to its supply chain, publishing a list of its global suppliers and factories on its website.

385.

The company has partnered with NGOs and local communities to support conservation efforts and protect biodiversity in regions where it operates.

386.

Patagonia has used its platform to raise awareness about pressing environmental issues, collaborating with artists and influencers to amplify their messages.

387.

The company has been an advocate for responsible consumption, encouraging customers to think about the environmental and social impacts of their purchasing decisions.

388.

Patagonia has implemented innovative recycling programs, such as its "Common Threads" initiative, which encourages customers to return their worn-out garments for recycling.

389.

The company has been recognized as a leader in corporate governance, with a commitment to transparency, accountability, and responsible decision-making.

390.

Patagonia has a strong commitment to diversity and inclusion, striving to create a more equitable and inclusive outdoor industry.

391.

The company has supported grassroots activism and community engagement through its Patagonia Action Works program, connecting individuals with local environmental organizations.

392.

Patagonia has launched initiatives to address the issue of microplastics in the oceans, working with scientists and partners to find solutions.

393.

The company has been involved in public policy advocacy, lobbying for stronger environmental regulations and supporting initiatives to address climate change.

394.

Patagonia has a dedicated team of environmental and social responsibility experts who work to ensure the company's practices align with its values and mission.

395.

The company has received widespread recognition for its commitment to corporate responsibility, earning accolades such as being named one of the World's Most Ethical Companies.

396.

Patagonia has taken steps to reduce waste in its packaging and shipping materials, using recycled and biodegradable materials whenever possible.

397.

The company has promoted sustainable farming practices through initiatives like its Regenerative Organic Certification, which focuses on soil health and biodiversity.

398.

Patagonia has supported grassroots conservation efforts in regions such as the Amazon rainforest, working to protect critical ecosystems and support indigenous communities.

399.

The company has been a leader in responsible supply chain management, conducting audits and assessments to ensure suppliers meet ethical and environmental standards.

400.

Patagonia's commitment to the environment goes beyond its business operations, as it has pledged to donate at least 1% of its annual sales to environmental causes through the 1% for the Planet initiative.

401.

The Silas Deane House is a historic mansion located in Wethersfield, Connecticut, built in 1766.

402.

It was originally the home of Silas Deane, a prominent figure in the American Revolutionary War and a delegate to the Continental Congress.

403.

The house is a fine example of Georgian architecture, characterized by its symmetrical design, decorative details, and balanced proportions.

404.

Silas Deane played a crucial role in securing French support for the American Revolution, and the house served as a meeting place for diplomatic discussions during that time.

405.

The house was one of the first brick mansions built in Connecticut and is considered a significant architectural landmark.

406.

The mansion features a central hallway with rooms on either side, including a formal parlor, dining room, and bedrooms.

407.

The interior of the Silas Deane House is adorned with period furnishings and artwork, providing a glimpse into the lifestyle of the colonial elite.

408.

Silas Deane's connections to influential figures of the time, such as Benjamin Franklin and Thomas Jefferson, likely influenced the design and grandeur of the house.

409.

The house served as the headquarters for General George Washington during the Revolutionary War when he planned the campaign against the British in New York.

410.

After Silas Deane's death, the house changed hands multiple times and served various purposes, including as a boarding house and a girls' school.

411.

The Silas Deane House was designated a National Historic Landmark in 1965 for its architectural significance and historical association with the Revolutionary War.

412.

The house is now a museum operated by the Connecticut Society of the Sons of the American Revolution, showcasing period artifacts and exhibits related to the American Revolution.

413.

The museum offers guided tours that provide visitors with insights into the life and times of Silas Deane and the significance of the house during the Revolutionary War.

414.

The Silas Deane House has been meticulously restored to its original appearance, allowing visitors to experience the grandeur of a colonial-era mansion.

415.

The house's architecture reflects the influence of European design trends, particularly English Georgian style, popular during the 18th century.

416.

The mansion features a distinctive gambrel roof, a characteristic of many colonial-era buildings in New England.

417.

Silas Deane was a successful merchant and diplomat, and his residence showcased his wealth and social status.

418.

The house's location in Wethersfield, one of the oldest towns in Connecticut, adds to its historical significance.

419.

Silas Deane's involvement in politics and his role in shaping American history make the house an important site for understanding the Revolutionary War era.

420.

The Silas Deane House has been the subject of archaeological research, uncovering artifacts that provide further insights into the daily life of its occupants.

421.

The house has been featured in several publications and documentaries focusing on American history and architecture.

422.

The Silas Deane House is surrounded by beautifully landscaped gardens that reflect the colonial-era style and enhance the overall ambiance of the property.

423.

The museum offers educational programs and events for visitors of all ages, including lectures, workshops, and living history demonstrations.

424.

The Silas Deane House serves as a venue for special events, such as weddings, receptions, and corporate functions, providing a unique and historic setting.

425.

The house's architectural details, such as its decorative molding, intricate woodwork, and period-style furnishings, exemplify the craftsmanship of the time.

426.

The property's historical significance extends beyond its association with Silas Deane, as it is also connected to other notable figures of the Revolutionary War period.

427.

The Silas Deane House is an important stop on historical tours of Connecticut, offering visitors a chance to delve into the state's colonial past.

428.

The house is known for its well-preserved original features, including its fireplaces, paneling, and original doors and hardware.

429.

Silas Deane's role as a diplomat and his efforts to secure French aid for the American cause played a pivotal role in the success of the Revolution.

430.

The house's location near the Connecticut River allowed for easy access to trade routes and transportation, contributing to Silas Deane's commercial success.

431.

The Silas Deane House is a testament to the wealth and prosperity enjoyed by some colonists, as well as their connections to the broader world.

432.

The house's exterior has been meticulously maintained, ensuring that its architectural integrity remains intact.

433.

The museum offers educational programs specifically tailored to school groups, providing a hands-on learning experience in a historical setting.

434.

The Silas Deane House provides a glimpse into the lifestyle of the colonial elite, showcasing their tastes in art, furnishings, and decor.

435.

The house's proximity to other historic sites in Connecticut, such as Old Wethersfield Historic District, makes it an ideal stop for history enthusiasts.

436.

The Silas Deane House is an important reminder of the sacrifices made by individuals like Deane, who played a vital role in the fight for American independence.

437.

The museum regularly collaborates with other historical organizations and institutions to offer a comprehensive understanding of the Revolutionary War period.

438.

The Silas Deane House is known for its welcoming atmosphere and knowledgeable staff, providing a memorable visitor experience.

439.

The property's preservation and maintenance are supported by a dedicated group of volunteers who work tirelessly to ensure its historical integrity.

440.

The museum's exhibits showcase the personal and political life of Silas Deane, shedding light on his contributions to the formation of the United States.

441.

The Silas Deane House is an excellent example of how historical structures can be repurposed and preserved for educational and cultural purposes.

442.

The house's location in the heart of Wethersfield allows visitors to explore the town's rich history, including its colonial-era architecture and charming Main Street.

443.

The Silas Deane House offers a unique perspective on the social, economic, and political landscape of the American Revolutionary War period.

444.

The museum regularly hosts special events and programming that celebrate American history and engage the local community.

445.

The Silas Deane House has been featured in television shows and documentaries focusing on American history and the Revolutionary War.

446.

The house's interior design reflects the tastes and trends of the 18th century, showcasing period furniture, artwork, and decorative items.

447.

The museum's collection includes a wide range of artifacts related to the Revolutionary War, providing a comprehensive understanding of the era.

448.

The Silas Deane House has been a source of inspiration for artists and writers, serving as a backdrop for creative works that capture the spirit of the American Revolution.

449.

The museum offers educational resources for teachers and students, including lesson plans, educational kits, and virtual programs.

450.

The Silas Deane House stands as a testament to the enduring legacy of the American Revolution and the individuals who shaped the nation's history.

451.

The Oliver Ellsworth Homestead is a historic house located in Windsor, Connecticut, built in 1781.

452.

The house was the birthplace and childhood home of Oliver Ellsworth, a prominent figure in early American politics and the third Chief Justice of the United States Supreme Court.

453.

The Ellsworth Homestead is a fine example of Georgian architecture, characterized by its symmetrical design, large windows, and central entrance.

454.

The house features a central hallway with rooms on either side, including a formal parlor, dining room, and bedrooms.

455.

Oliver Ellsworth played a significant role in shaping the United States Constitution and was instrumental in the formation of the federal judiciary system.

456.

The Ellsworth Homestead is a designated National Historic Landmark and is listed on the National Register of Historic Places for its architectural and historical significance.

457.

The house is open to the public as a museum and offers guided tours that provide insights into the life and times of Oliver Ellsworth and his contributions to American history.

458.

The interior of the house is furnished with period pieces and artifacts, allowing visitors to experience the ambiance of a late 18th-century New England home.

459.

The Ellsworth Homestead showcases the lifestyle of a prominent colonial-era family, reflecting their social status and wealth.

460.

The house's architecture reflects the influence of English design trends of the time, with its symmetrical facade and refined details.

461.

The Ellsworth Homestead remained in the Ellsworth family for several generations before being acquired by the Connecticut Daughters of the American Revolution.

462.

The museum offers educational programs and exhibits that explore the life and legacy of Oliver Ellsworth and the early years of the United States.

463.

The Ellsworth Homestead is located in close proximity to other historic sites in Windsor, such as the First Church of Windsor and the Palisado Green, offering visitors a rich historical experience.

464.

The house has been meticulously restored to its original appearance, allowing visitors to step back in time and learn about the daily life of a prominent colonial family.

465.

Oliver Ellsworth's contributions to the founding of the nation are highlighted in the museum, providing a deeper understanding of the political climate of the late 18th century.

466.

The Ellsworth Homestead is a popular destination for history enthusiasts, researchers, and students interested in early American history and the United States Constitution.

467.

The house's location in Windsor, one of the oldest towns in Connecticut, adds to its historical significance and provides a sense of the area's colonial heritage.

468.

The Ellsworth family played a role in various aspects of early American history, including politics, law, and military service.

469.

The museum offers special events and programs throughout the year, such as lectures, reenactments, and historical demonstrations, providing an immersive experience for visitors.

470.

The Ellsworth Homestead serves as a venue for community events, weddings, and other private functions, offering a unique and historic setting.

471.

The house's garden and grounds are meticulously maintained and reflect the horticultural practices of the 18th century, featuring period-appropriate plants and landscaping.

472.

The Ellsworth Homestead is associated with significant moments in American history, including the adoption of the United States Constitution and the establishment of the federal court system.

473.

The museum showcases artifacts and documents related to Oliver Ellsworth's life and career, including personal belongings, correspondence, and legal manuscripts.

474.

The house's architecture and design elements reflect the changing tastes and trends of the late 18th century, providing insights into the evolution of domestic architecture during that period.

475.

The Ellsworth Homestead is an important stop on historical tours of Connecticut, offering visitors a chance to explore the state's colonial past and its impact on the nation's history.

476.

The museum's collection includes portraits, furniture, and decorative arts from the 18th century, providing a visual representation of the time period.

477.

The Ellsworth Homestead has been featured in various publications and documentaries focusing on American history and colonial-era architecture.

478.

The house's proximity to the Connecticut River, a major transportation route in the colonial era, highlights the importance of waterways in early American settlement and trade.

479.

The museum offers interactive exhibits and activities for children, making it an engaging and educational experience for visitors of all ages.

480.

The Ellsworth Homestead is a well-preserved example of a colonial-era residence, showcasing the craftsmanship and attention to detail of the time.

481.

The house's historic significance extends beyond its association with Oliver Ellsworth, as it represents the broader history of Connecticut and its role in the formation of the United States.

482.

The museum collaborates with other historical organizations and institutions to provide a comprehensive understanding of the Revolutionary War era and the early years of the United States.

483.

The Ellsworth Homestead has been a source of inspiration for artists, writers, and scholars interested in American history and the founding principles of the nation.

484.

The house's location near the Connecticut River Valley offers visitors access to scenic landscapes and outdoor activities, enhancing their overall experience.

485.

The museum regularly hosts temporary exhibits that explore various aspects of early American history, providing fresh perspectives and engaging narratives.

486.

The Ellsworth Homestead is known for its knowledgeable and passionate staff, who are dedicated to preserving and sharing the history of the house and its significance.

487.

The museum offers online resources, including virtual tours and educational materials, allowing individuals from around the world to explore the Ellsworth Homestead's history.

488.

The house's architecture and construction methods reflect the materials and techniques used in colonial New England, highlighting the region's craftsmanship.

489.

The Ellsworth Homestead has been used as a filming location for movies and television shows that depict the colonial period and American history.

490.

The museum's gift shop offers a variety of books, souvenirs, and educational materials related to American history and the colonial era.

491.

The Ellsworth Homestead is a popular destination for school field trips, providing students with a hands-on learning experience in a historic setting.

492.

The museum actively collects and preserves artifacts and documents related to the Ellsworth family and their historical significance, ensuring their accessibility for future generations.

493.

The house's architectural features, such as its decorative molding, fireplaces, and period-style doors and windows, reflect the craftsmanship of the time.

494.

The museum conducts ongoing research and scholarship on the history of the Ellsworth family, contributing to a deeper understanding of their contributions to American history.

495.

The Ellsworth Homestead's location in a residential neighborhood allows visitors to experience the local community and explore the area's historic charm.

496.

The museum offers volunteer and internship opportunities, allowing individuals to gain firsthand experience in museum operations and preservation practices.

497.

The house's proximity to other cultural attractions and historical sites in Connecticut makes it an ideal stop for those interested in exploring the state's rich heritage.

498.

The Ellsworth Homestead has been recognized with awards and accolades for its preservation efforts and commitment to sharing the history of Oliver Ellsworth and his family.

499.

The museum actively engages with the local community through outreach programs, partnerships with schools, and collaborative initiatives with other cultural institutions.

500.

The Ellsworth Homestead serves as a valuable resource for researchers, historians, and genealogists interested in the Ellsworth family and their contributions to American history.

501.

The great white shark (Carcharodon carcharias) is a species of shark known for its large size, powerful jaws, and predatory behavior.

502.

It is one of the largest predatory fish species, with mature individuals reaching lengths of up to 20 feet (6 meters) and weighing over 5,000 pounds (2,268 kilograms).

503.

The great white shark has a unique torpedo-shaped body, dark gray or black on top and white on the underside, which helps it blend in with the ocean's depths and surface.

504.

These sharks have an excellent sense of smell and can detect even a small amount of blood in the water from miles away.

505.

Great white sharks are found in various coastal waters around the world, including the United States, South Africa, Australia, and New Zealand.

506.

They are apex predators and play a crucial role in maintaining the balance of marine ecosystems.

507.

The great white shark has rows of sharp, serrated teeth, which can number up to 300. These teeth are continually replaced throughout the shark's lifetime.

508.

They are known for their powerful bite, which can exert immense pressure, estimated to be around 4,000 pounds per square inch (psi).

509.

Great white sharks are primarily carnivorous and feed on a variety of marine animals, including seals, sea lions, fish, dolphins, and even other sharks.

510.

They are known for their unique hunting technique known as "breaching," where they launch themselves out of the water to surprise their prey.

511.

The great white shark is an excellent swimmer, capable of reaching speeds of up to 25 miles per hour (40 kilometers per hour).

512.

Despite their size and reputation as apex predators, great white sharks are not typically a threat to humans. Most attacks on humans are believed to be cases of mistaken identity.

513.

Great white sharks are generally solitary animals, but they can occasionally be seen in groups, especially during mating season or around abundant food sources.

514.

Mating in great white sharks occurs through internal fertilization, and females give birth to live young.

515.

The gestation period for great white sharks is estimated to be around 12 to 18 months, and a litter typically consists of 4 to 14 pups.

516.

Great white shark pups are born fully formed and are miniature versions of adults, measuring around 3 to 4 feet (1 to 1.2 meters) in length.

517.

These sharks have a long lifespan, with some individuals believed to live up to 70 years or more.

518.

Great white sharks have a specialized sense organ called the ampullae of Lorenzini, which allows them to detect electromagnetic fields generated by the movement of prey.

519.

The global population of great white sharks is currently declining due to overfishing, habitat loss, and accidental capture in fishing gear.

520.

Great white sharks are protected in many countries, and several conservation organizations work to promote their conservation and raise awareness about their importance in marine ecosystems.

521.

The first scientific description of the great white shark was made in 1758 by Swedish naturalist Carl Linnaeus.

522.

The great white shark is a popular subject in movies and literature, often portrayed as a fearsome predator and symbol of the ocean's mysteries.

523.

The largest great white shark ever recorded was an individual known as "Deep Blue," estimated to be around 20 feet (6 meters) in length. It was spotted off the coast of Guadalupe Island in Mexico.

524.

Great white sharks have been known to migrate over long distances, with some individuals traveling thousands of miles between feeding and breeding grounds.

525.

They have an extraordinary ability to detect electrical signals emitted by living organisms, helping them locate prey even in dark or murky waters.

526.

Great white sharks are known to breach the water surface during hunting or courtship displays, often launching their entire body into the air.

527.

The great white shark's liver accounts for a significant portion of its body weight and is rich in oil, which helps provide buoyancy and energy reserves.

528.

These sharks have a keen sense of hearing and can detect low-frequency sounds and vibrations, which aids in locating prey.

529.

Great white sharks are not just confined to saltwater habitats. They have been observed in brackish estuaries and even ventured into freshwater rivers on rare occasions.

530.

The population of great white sharks in the northeastern Pacific Ocean is estimated to be around 340 individuals, making it one of the most studied populations.

531.

Great white sharks have been known to scavenge on whale carcasses, taking advantage of the abundant food source.

532.

The great white shark's skin is covered in tiny tooth-like scales called dermal denticles, which reduce drag and increase swimming efficiency.

533.

Great white sharks have a reputation for their powerful bite, but they lack the ability to chew food. Instead, they rely on ripping and tearing their prey into manageable pieces.

534.

These sharks have a complex social structure, with dominant individuals establishing hierarchy within their groups.

535.

The great white shark's eyes are adapted for hunting in low-light conditions and can dilate to let in more light in dark waters.

536.

Great white sharks have been found with various types of parasites, including barnacles, copepods, and parasitic worms, attached to their bodies.

537.

The great white shark's brain is relatively small compared to its body size but is highly developed in areas responsible for sensory processing and motor coordination.

538.

The great white shark is considered a keystone species, meaning its presence and activities have a significant impact on the structure and function of its ecosystem.

539.

The teeth of a great white shark are continuously replaced throughout its life. A single shark can go through thousands of teeth during its lifetime.

540.

Great white sharks are capable of regulating their body temperature to some extent, allowing them to inhabit a wide range of ocean temperatures.

541.

The great white shark's skeleton is composed mainly of cartilage, which is lighter and more flexible than bone, enabling faster swimming.

542.

These sharks have a highly developed sense of touch, particularly in their snout, which helps them locate and investigate potential prey.

543.

Great white sharks have been observed displaying curiosity and investigatory behavior towards unfamiliar objects, including boats and divers.

544.

The great white shark's liver plays a crucial role in buoyancy control. It contains large amounts of oil that help offset the shark's density in water.

545.

Great white sharks have a unique hunting strategy called "spy hopping," where they raise their heads out of the water to survey their surroundings and locate potential prey.

546.

The great white shark's impressive size and appearance have made it a popular subject for wildlife documentaries and research expeditions.

547.

These sharks have a strong sense of territoriality and may display aggressive behavior towards other sharks that encroach on their feeding grounds.

548.

Great white sharks are known for their ability to breach the water surface while hunting, a behavior that is often seen in regions with seal colonies.

549.

The great white shark's sense of smell is highly developed and allows it to detect even trace amounts of blood in the water.

550.

The conservation status of the great white shark is currently listed as vulnerable by the International Union for Conservation of Nature (IUCN), highlighting the need for conservation efforts to protect this iconic species.

551.

The greater flamingo (Phoenicopterus roseus) is the largest species of flamingo and is known for its vibrant pink feathers and long, graceful neck.

552.

They are found in various parts of the world, including parts of Africa, Europe, Asia, and the Americas.

553.

The average adult greater flamingo stands around 4 to 5 feet (1.2 to 1.5 meters) tall and can weigh between 4.4 to 8.8 pounds (2 to 4 kilograms).

554.

Their distinctive pink color comes from pigments in the shrimp and algae they consume, which contain carotenoids.

555.

Greater flamingos have a wingspan of about 4 to 5 feet (1.2 to 1.5 meters), allowing them to gracefully glide through the air.

556.

They have long, thin legs with webbed feet that are adapted for wading through shallow water.

557.

These birds have a flexible, downward-curving beak with a filter-feeding structure that allows them to strain small organisms and algae from the water.

558.

Flamingos are social birds and live in large colonies, often numbering in the thousands.

559.

They communicate through various vocalizations, including honking and growling sounds.

560.

Greater flamingos are monogamous, and pairs bond for life. They perform elaborate courtship displays, including synchronized dancing and head-flagging.

561.

The breeding season of greater flamingos varies depending on their location, but it generally occurs during the wet season when food availability is high.

562.

They construct mud nests in shallow water or on islands, and both parents take turns incubating the eggs.

563.

The incubation period for greater flamingo eggs is around 28 to 32 days.

564.

Flamingo chicks are initially gray or white in color and develop their pink feathers over time as they consume a diet rich in carotenoids.

565.

The parents feed their young chicks with a specialized secretion called "crop milk," which is produced in their upper digestive tract.

566.

Greater flamingos are known for their unique feeding behavior called "filter feeding." They submerge their heads upside down in the water and filter out small organisms and algae using their specialized beak.

567.

Flamingos are excellent swimmers and use their webbed feet to paddle through the water.

568.

They can often be seen standing on one leg, which helps them conserve body heat and maintain balance.

569.

The average lifespan of a greater flamingo is around 20 to 30 years in the wild, although some individuals have been known to live up to 50 years.

570.

Greater flamingos are highly adaptable and can thrive in a variety of habitats, including saltwater lagoons, estuaries, mudflats, and alkaline or saline lakes.

571.

Flamingos have a unique circulatory system that allows them to regulate body temperature. They can increase or decrease blood flow to their legs to adjust to hot or cold conditions.

572.

The greater flamingo is listed as a species of least concern by the International Union for Conservation of Nature (IUCN) due to its wide distribution and stable population.

573.

Flamingos play a vital role in the ecosystem by filtering algae and small organisms from the water, which helps maintain water quality and balance nutrient levels.

574.

They are considered an umbrella species, meaning their conservation benefits many other species in their habitat.

575.

Greater flamingos are highly gregarious and often engage in synchronized feeding, where large groups move together in unison.

576.

The flight of flamingos is characterized by their long, outstretched necks and steady, rhythmic wingbeats.

577.

They are excellent fliers and can reach speeds of up to 35 miles per hour (56 kilometers per hour) in flight.

578.

Flamingos have few natural predators, but they may be preyed upon by large birds of prey, such as eagles or vultures.

579.

The word "flamingo" is derived from the Spanish word "flamenco," which means flame-colored.

580.

Flamingos have a unique adaptation in their beak that allows them to filter-feed while keeping their head upside down in the water.

581.

The greater flamingo has a complex visual system that allows it to detect colors and perceive depth accurately.

582.

Flamingos have a dense plumage that helps insulate them from both cold and hot temperatures.

583.

During mating season, male flamingos perform intricate courtship displays that involve head-turning, wing-spreading, and synchronized marching.

584.

Flamingos can sleep while standing on one leg, with half of their brain remaining alert to potential threats.

585.

The plumage of greater flamingos is not naturally pink. It is the result of their diet rich in carotenoids, which are converted into pigments responsible for their vibrant coloration.

586.

Flamingos engage in communal nest-building, with multiple nests clustered close together in a group.

587.

Greater flamingos are capable of flying long distances in search of suitable breeding and feeding grounds.

588.

Flamingos have a specialized gland near their tail called the uropygial gland, which produces oil that they use to preen and waterproof their feathers.

589.

Flamingos have a unique method of cooling down in hot weather. They can partially submerge themselves in water and splash it onto their bodies to regulate their body temperature.

590.

Greater flamingos have a high salt tolerance and can live in habitats with high salinity levels that are inhospitable to other species.

591.

Flamingos are known to engage in "marches" where they move in a line, often in shallow water, creating a visually stunning spectacle.

592.

In ancient Egypt, flamingos were considered sacred birds and were depicted in various artworks and hieroglyphics.

593.

Flamingos have a long, flexible neck that allows them to reach down into the water to feed while keeping their body upright.

594.

Flamingos have a unique reproductive strategy. They lay a single egg, and both parents take turns incubating it and caring for the chick.

595.

The diet of greater flamingos consists mainly of algae, diatoms, crustaceans, small fish, and insects found in shallow water.

596.

Flamingos are excellent vocalizers and communicate through a variety of calls, including honks, grunts, and trumpeting sounds.

597.

The bill of a flamingo contains numerous sensory receptors that help them detect prey in muddy or murky water.

598.

Flamingos engage in "wing-flagging" behavior, where they extend one wing out and move it in a circular motion as part of their courtship displays.

599.

Flamingos have been featured in art, literature, and folklore throughout history, symbolizing grace, beauty, and elegance.

600.

The collective noun for a group of flamingos is a "flamboyance," which aptly describes the stunning display of these magnificent birds when seen together.

601.

Chevrolet was founded on November 3, 1911, by Louis Chevrolet and William C. Durant.

602.

The first Chevrolet car, the Classic Six, was introduced in 1912.

603.

In 1915, Chevrolet was merged with General Motors (GM) and became a division of the company.

604.

The iconic Chevrolet bowtie logo was introduced in 1913 and has since become one of the most recognizable automotive logos.

605.

Chevrolet produced its first truck, the Chevrolet Model 490 Light Delivery, in 1918.

606.

Chevrolet played a crucial role in World War II by producing military vehicles, aircraft engines, and artillery shells.

607.

The Chevrolet Bel Air, introduced in 1950, became one of the most popular and iconic cars of the 1950s and 1960s.

608.

In 1953, Chevrolet introduced the first Corvette, a two-seat sports car that quickly became an American classic.

609.

The Chevrolet Impala, introduced in 1958, became one of the best-selling cars in the United States.

610.

Chevrolet introduced the first small-block V8 engine in 1955, which revolutionized the automotive industry and became the basis for many subsequent engines.

611.

The Chevrolet Camaro was introduced in 1966 as a direct competitor to the Ford Mustang, igniting a long-lasting rivalry between the two iconic American muscle cars.

612.

Chevrolet introduced the first electric vehicle (EV) in its lineup, the
Chevrolet Volt, in 2010.

613.

In 2017, Chevrolet launched the Bolt EV, a fully electric vehicle
with an impressive range of over 200 miles (322 kilometers).

614.

Chevrolet has a rich history in motorsports, including NASCAR,
where the brand has won numerous championships and races.

615.

Chevrolet has also had success in other forms of motorsports, such
as IndyCar and endurance racing, including multiple wins at the 24
Hours of Le Mans.

616.

Chevrolet's pickup trucks, including the Silverado and Colorado,
have been consistently popular and have earned a reputation for their
durability and capability.

617.

Chevrolet has been at the forefront of automotive innovation,
introducing features such as power steering, power brakes, and air
conditioning in its vehicles.

618.

In 1979, Chevrolet introduced the Malibu, a midsize car that has
become one of the brand's longest-running nameplates.

619.

Chevrolet has been recognized for its safety innovations, with many
of its vehicles receiving high safety ratings and incorporating
advanced safety features.

620.

Chevrolet has a global presence, with vehicles sold in over 140 countries.

621.

Chevrolet has been involved in numerous philanthropic efforts, supporting initiatives such as education, youth programs, and environmental sustainability.

622.

Chevrolet's lineup includes a wide range of vehicles, from compact cars to SUVs and trucks, catering to diverse customer needs and preferences.

623.

Chevrolet has embraced alternative fuel technologies, offering vehicles powered by compressed natural gas (CNG), ethanol, and hydrogen fuel cells.

624.

The Chevrolet Corvette has a storied history in sports car racing, with numerous victories at events such as the 24 Hours of Daytona and the 12 Hours of Sebring.

625.

Chevrolet has collaborated with various artists and designers over the years to create special edition vehicles, showcasing unique styling and features.

626.

Chevrolet introduced the first production car with built-in Wi-Fi hotspot capability, allowing passengers to stay connected on the go.

627.

Chevrolet has been recognized for its commitment to environmental
sustainability, implementing measures to reduce carbon emissions
and promote energy efficiency.

628.

Chevrolet has a strong presence in the global market, with
manufacturing facilities in several countries, including the United
States, Mexico, Canada, and China.

629.

Chevrolet has received numerous awards and accolades throughout
its history, including recognition for vehicle quality, reliability, and
customer satisfaction.

630.

Chevrolet has a dedicated fan base and enthusiast community, with
events and gatherings held worldwide to celebrate the brand's
heritage and iconic vehicles.

631.

Chevrolet has supported various charitable organizations and
initiatives, such as the American Cancer Society and the United
Way.

632.

Chevrolet has a long-standing commitment to performance, with
vehicles like the Chevrolet Camaro ZL1 and Corvette ZR1
delivering exhilarating driving experiences.

633.

Chevrolet has introduced several concept cars over the years,
showcasing advanced technologies and design innovations that may
influence future production models.

634.

Chevrolet has embraced connectivity and infotainment features, offering systems such as Chevrolet MyLink that integrate smartphones and provide enhanced entertainment and navigation capabilities.

635.

Chevrolet has a rich heritage of advertising campaigns, including memorable slogans such as "See the USA in Your Chevrolet" and "Like a Rock."

636.

Chevrolet has expanded its global reach, introducing vehicles tailored to specific markets and regions, including the Chevrolet Onix in South America and the Chevrolet Captiva in Asia.

637.

Chevrolet has been recognized for its commitment to diversity and inclusion, with initiatives aimed at fostering a diverse workforce and promoting equality.

638.

Chevrolet has partnered with various organizations and institutions to advance STEM education and inspire the next generation of engineers and innovators.

639.

Chevrolet has a strong presence in the electric vehicle market, with the introduction of the Chevrolet Bolt EV and upcoming electric models planned for the future.

640.

Chevrolet has embraced autonomous driving technology, investing in research and development to enhance vehicle safety and driver-assistance features.

641.

Chevrolet has a long-standing commitment to manufacturing quality, with rigorous testing and inspection processes to ensure customer satisfaction.

642.

Chevrolet has introduced hybrid and plug-in hybrid models, offering customers more fuel-efficient options without sacrificing performance.

643.

Chevrolet has a rich motorsports heritage, with victories in iconic races such as the Indianapolis 500 and the Daytona 500.

644.

Chevrolet has been recognized for its commitment to customer service, offering programs such as Chevrolet Complete Care, which includes maintenance, warranty coverage, and roadside assistance.

645.

Chevrolet has a strong presence in the truck market, with the Silverado lineup known for its ruggedness, capability, and innovative features.

646.

Chevrolet has embraced advanced driver-assistance systems (ADAS), offering features such as adaptive cruise control, lane-keeping assist, and automatic emergency braking.

647.

Chevrolet has a legacy of innovation in vehicle design, with iconic models such as the Chevrolet Corvette Stingray known for their aerodynamic styling and performance-oriented features.

648.

Chevrolet has a rich racing heritage, with involvement in various forms of motorsports, including drag racing, rally racing, and sports car racing.

649.

Chevrolet has introduced electric vehicle charging infrastructure initiatives, working with partners to expand the availability and accessibility of charging stations.

650.

Chevrolet continues to evolve and innovate, embracing emerging technologies and trends to meet the needs and preferences of modern customers.

651.

Weight Watchers was founded in 1963 by Jean Nidetch, a housewife from Queens, New York.

652.

The company initially started as a support group for Nidetch and her friends to help each other lose weight.

653.

The first official Weight Watchers meeting took place in Nidetch's living room with just a handful of attendees.

654.

The program gained popularity quickly, and by 1968, Weight Watchers had over 100,000 members.

655.

In 1978, Weight Watchers became a publicly traded company on the New York Stock Exchange.

656.

Weight Watchers introduced its Points system in 1997, which assigned a point value to different foods based on their nutritional content.

657.

The Points system revolutionized the way people approached dieting, as it allowed for flexibility and personal choices within a structured framework.

658.

In 2000, Weight Watchers launched its online program, offering members access to tools, resources, and support through the internet.

659.

Weight Watchers expanded globally, with programs available in over 30 countries, including Canada, the United Kingdom, Australia, and Germany.

660.

In 2015, Weight Watchers introduced the Beyond the Scale program, focusing on overall wellness and lifestyle changes rather than just weight loss.

661.

Weight Watchers rebranded itself as WW in 2018, shifting its focus to wellness and holistic health.

662.

The company introduced the myWW program in 2019, which offers members three different customized plans to suit their individual needs and preferences.

663.

Celebrities such as Oprah Winfrey and DJ Khaled have publicly endorsed and partnered with Weight Watchers, sharing their weight loss journeys with the brand.

664.

Weight Watchers has a strong emphasis on community and support, with weekly meetings and online forums where members can share their experiences and receive encouragement.

665.

The company has a team of registered dietitians and nutritionists who provide guidance and education to members.

666.

Weight Watchers has been recognized for its science-backed approach to weight loss, with a focus on balanced nutrition, portion control, and behavior change.

667.

The Weight Watchers program encourages physical activity and offers guidance on incorporating exercise into a healthy lifestyle.

668.

The company has embraced technology, developing mobile apps and wearables that help members track their food intake, activity levels, and progress.

669.

Weight Watchers has partnered with major food and beverage brands to create and promote healthier, lower-calorie options.

670.

The company has published numerous cookbooks and recipe guides to inspire and support healthy eating.

671.

Weight Watchers has a long-standing commitment to research and development, continuously evolving its program based on the latest scientific findings.

672.

The company has received accolades for its corporate social responsibility efforts, including sustainability initiatives and charitable partnerships.

673.

Weight Watchers has been at the forefront of promoting body positivity and self-acceptance, encouraging members to focus on overall well-being rather than just the number on the scale.

674.

The company has a network of trained coaches who provide personalized support and guidance to help members achieve their weight loss goals.

675.

Weight Watchers has been involved in community outreach programs, offering free resources and education to underserved populations.

676.

The company has a strong online presence, with social media platforms and digital communities where members can connect and share their success stories.

677.

Weight Watchers has been recognized by health organizations and experts for its evidence-based approach to weight loss and healthy living.

678.

The company offers specialized programs for different life stages and health conditions, such as Weight Watchers for Diabetes and Weight Watchers for Breastfeeding.

679.

Weight Watchers has expanded its offerings beyond weight loss, with programs focused on specific goals like maintaining weight, improving fitness, and managing stress.

680.

The company has a history of adapting to changing consumer preferences and dietary trends, offering options for vegetarian, vegan, and gluten-free diets.

681.

Weight Watchers has conducted clinical studies to demonstrate the effectiveness of its program in achieving sustainable weight loss.

682.

The company has a strong online presence, with a blog, articles, and success stories that provide inspiration and education to members and the public.

683.

Weight Watchers has a loyalty program called WellnessWins, which rewards members for their healthy habits and achievements.

684.

The company has embraced technology advancements, such as incorporating artificial intelligence and machine learning into its digital platforms.

685.

Weight Watchers has been involved in advocacy efforts to promote policies that support healthy eating, nutrition education, and obesity prevention.

686.

The company has a comprehensive approach to wellness, addressing not only diet and exercise but also sleep, stress management, and mindfulness.

687.

Weight Watchers has a long history of partnering with healthcare providers and insurance companies to offer weight management programs as part of preventive care.

688.

The company has a robust research and development team that continually evaluates and updates its program based on scientific evidence.

689.

Weight Watchers has been recognized as a top employer, providing opportunities for career growth and professional development.

690.

The company offers a range of digital tools and resources, including recipe builders, meal planners, and virtual workshops, to enhance the member experience.

691.

Weight Watchers has been involved in community initiatives, such as school programs and workplace wellness campaigns, to promote healthier lifestyles.

692.

The company has a network of trained leaders who facilitate meetings and provide guidance and support to members.

693.

Weight Watchers has a strong focus on behavior change and offers resources to help members develop healthier habits and mindset.

694.

The company has a mobile app that allows members to track their progress, access recipes and meal ideas, and connect with other members for support and motivation.

695.

Weight Watchers has a rewards program called Wins, where members can earn points for activities such as tracking their meals, attending workshops, and achieving weight loss milestones.

696.

The company has been at the forefront of using data analytics to personalize the member experience and offer tailored recommendations.

697.

Weight Watchers has a corporate wellness program that partners with companies to provide weight management and wellness solutions to employees.

698.

The company has a long-standing commitment to inclusivity and offers resources and support for individuals of all backgrounds, body types, and dietary preferences.

699.

Weight Watchers has a research advisory board comprised of leading experts in the fields of nutrition, obesity, and behavior change.

700.

The company has a comprehensive maintenance program to help members sustain their weight loss and adopt long-term healthy habits.

701.

The Emma C. Berry is a historic fishing vessel that was built in 1866 in Noank, Connecticut.

702.

The boat was constructed by Charles Mallory and was named after his daughter, Emma C. Berry.

703.

The Emma C. Berry is a traditional Eastern-rigged sailing vessel used for fishing in the Long Island Sound.

704.

The boat was primarily used for the local fishery, targeting species such as cod, haddock, and flounder.

705.

The Emma C. Berry is a sloop-rigged vessel, meaning it has a single mast with a fore-and-aft rigged sail.

706.

The boat measures 45 feet in length and has a beam of 13 feet.

707.

The Emma C. Berry is built of wood, with a sturdy hull and a distinctive green-painted exterior.

708.

The vessel has a flat bottom, which allows it to navigate in shallow waters and work close to the shore.

709.

The Emma C. Berry originally used oars and sails for propulsion, but it was later equipped with an engine for increased efficiency.

710.

The boat's design and construction reflect the traditional fishing methods and craftsmanship of the late 19th century.

711.

The Emma C. Berry has been recognized as a National Historic Landmark, preserving its cultural and historical significance.

712.

The vessel has undergone several restorations over the years to ensure its preservation and seaworthiness.

713.

The Emma C. Berry is still actively used for educational and recreational purposes, offering sailing trips and historical tours.

714.

The vessel provides a unique opportunity for visitors to experience the maritime heritage of New England.

715.

The Emma C. Berry has participated in various maritime festivals and events, showcasing its historical significance.

716.

The boat's design and rigging make it well-suited for sailing in the coastal waters of the Atlantic.

717.

The Emma C. Berry has a rich history, with many stories and legends associated with its fishing adventures.

718.

The vessel has inspired artists, photographers, and writers who appreciate its beauty and historical significance.

719.

The Emma C. Berry is a symbol of the maritime heritage and fishing traditions of the New England region.

720.

The boat has been featured in documentaries and films highlighting the history of fishing in the area.

721.

The Emma C. Berry has been sailed by skilled fishermen who have passed down their knowledge and expertise through generations.

722.

The vessel represents a time when fishing was a vital industry, providing sustenance and livelihoods for coastal communities.

723.

The Emma C. Berry has weathered storms and rough seas, showcasing its durability and seaworthiness.

724.

The boat has been owned and operated by different individuals and organizations dedicated to its preservation and promotion.

725.

The Emma C. Berry has been studied and documented by maritime historians and enthusiasts interested in its construction and history.

726.

The vessel's distinct green color is often associated with its identity and is recognized by those familiar with the boat.

727.

The Emma C. Berry is a reminder of the challenges and rewards of traditional fishing methods, contrasting with modern industrial practices.

728.

The boat has served as a training platform for aspiring sailors and fishermen, imparting traditional skills and knowledge.

729.

The Emma C. Berry has been an inspiration for other boat builders and enthusiasts interested in traditional vessel construction.

730.

The vessel has been a subject of admiration and fascination for those with an interest in maritime history and culture.

731.

The Emma C. Berry has been featured in maritime museums and exhibits, allowing visitors to learn about its significance.

732.

The boat has a unique character and charm, with its wooden structure and classic sailing design.

733.

The Emma C. Berry has a connection to the local community, representing the heritage and identity of the fishing industry.

734.

The vessel's presence on the water evokes a sense of nostalgia and transports observers to a bygone era.

735.

The boat's craftsmanship and attention to detail highlight the skills and dedication of its builders.

736.

The Emma C. Berry has been a source of pride for the individuals and organizations involved in its preservation and maintenance.

737.

The vessel's historical value extends beyond its physical structure, encompassing the stories and memories associated with its use.

738.

The boat has been a source of inspiration for those interested in maritime traditions and cultural preservation.

739.

The Emma C. Berry has been a subject of study for naval architects and historians examining the evolution of fishing vessel designs.

740.

The vessel has been a part of community celebrations and parades, showcasing its cultural importance.

741.

The boat's sailing capabilities and maneuverability make it a versatile vessel for educational and recreational purposes.

742.

The Emma C. Berry has been featured in books, articles, and documentaries exploring the history of traditional fishing methods.

743.

The vessel's restoration and maintenance require specialized knowledge and expertise in traditional boatbuilding techniques.

744.

The boat has participated in regattas and races, demonstrating its speed and agility on the water.

745.

The Emma C. Berry has been recognized for its contribution to the preservation of the maritime heritage of Noank, Connecticut.

746.

The vessel serves as a reminder of the close connection between humans and the sea, as well as the dependence on the ocean's resources.

747.

The boat's historical significance extends beyond its local community, representing a broader cultural heritage of coastal regions.

748.

The Emma C. Berry has become a symbol of resilience and tradition, standing the test of time and continuing to sail the waters.

749.

The vessel's historical documentation, including photographs and written accounts, provides valuable insights into the fishing practices of the past.

750.

The Emma C. Berry invites visitors and enthusiasts to step aboard and experience a piece of living history, honoring the legacy of the local fishing industry.

751.

The First Church of Christ, also known as the Center Church, is located in Hartford, Connecticut.

752.

The church was founded in 1632, making it one of the oldest continuously active congregations in the United States.

753.

The original church building was constructed in 1641 and was located on the site of the present-day church.

754.

The current church building, designed in the Greek Revival style, was built in 1807 and is listed on the National Register of Historic Places.

755.

The church's congregation played a significant role in the establishment of the Connecticut Colony and the early development of Hartford.

756.

The Center Church has a rich history closely intertwined with the history of Connecticut and the United States.

757.

The church building has undergone several renovations and restorations over the years to preserve its historic integrity.

758.

The steeple of the church stands at 196 feet tall and is a prominent landmark in downtown Hartford.

759.

The Center Church is known for its beautiful stained glass windows, including the historic Tiffany stained glass window depicting the Last Supper.

760.

The church's interior features impressive architectural details, including a grand pulpit and intricate woodwork.

761.

The First Church of Christ is a member of the United Church of Christ denomination.

762.

The church has a strong commitment to community service and social justice, actively engaging in various outreach programs.

763.

The Center Church has a vibrant music program, including a renowned choir and regular musical performances.

764.

The church's cemetery, known as the Ancient Burying Ground, is one of the oldest in Hartford and contains the graves of many prominent historical figures.

765.

The Center Church played a significant role in the development of the Hartford School of the Arts, a renowned performing arts high school.

766.

The church has been a gathering place for important community events and has hosted notable speakers and leaders throughout history.

767.

The Center Church has a strong commitment to education and has been involved in the establishment and support of various educational institutions.

768.

The church has a rich tradition of preaching and theological scholarship, with many notable pastors and theologians serving its congregation.

769.

The Center Church has a diverse and inclusive congregation, welcoming people from all walks of life.

770.

The church has been a source of spiritual guidance and support for its members and the wider community for centuries.

771.

The First Church of Christ has embraced modern technology, utilizing social media and online platforms to connect with its members and share its message.

772.

The church hosts regular worship services, as well as educational programs, Bible studies, and community events.

773.

The Center Church has been involved in various social and political movements throughout history, advocating for equality and justice.

774.

The church building is an architectural gem, featuring beautiful columns, a grand entrance, and a striking façade.

775.

The Center Church's archives contain a wealth of historical documents and artifacts, offering valuable insights into the history of Hartford and the church itself.

776.

The church has strong ties to the arts community, supporting local artists and hosting exhibitions and performances.

777.

The Center Church has been recognized for its commitment to environmental stewardship, implementing sustainable practices and advocating for conservation efforts.

778.

The church's congregation actively engages in interfaith dialogue and cooperation, fostering relationships with other religious communities.

779.

The Center Church has a strong sense of tradition and continues to uphold its historical values while adapting to the changing needs of its congregation.

780.

The church has a strong commitment to youth and family ministries, providing programs and support for children, teenagers, and parents.

781.

The First Church of Christ has a deep sense of community, offering fellowship opportunities and creating a welcoming space for all.

782.

The church has played a role in the preservation and promotion of Hartford's cultural heritage, supporting local museums and historical sites.

783.

The Center Church has been a center for learning and intellectual discourse, hosting lectures, seminars, and educational events.

784.

The church's archives contain a collection of historical artifacts, including early Bibles, sermons, and correspondence of notable church members.

785.

The Center Church has been a place of solace and support during times of crisis, offering counseling services and pastoral care.

786.

The church's annual Christmas pageant is a cherished tradition, bringing together members of all ages to celebrate the holiday season.

787.

The Center Church has actively supported initiatives for social and economic justice, addressing issues such as poverty, racism, and inequality.

788.

The church has a commitment to global missions, supporting international relief efforts and partnering with churches around the world.

789.

The First Church of Christ has a deep appreciation for the arts, hosting concerts, recitals, and art exhibitions.

790.

The church's historical significance has been recognized by the Hartford community, with plaques and markers commemorating its role in the city's history.

791.

The Center Church has been a catalyst for positive change in Hartford, actively engaging with community organizations and advocating for social progress.

792.

The church's bell tower houses a historic bell that has been rung to mark significant events and occasions throughout history.

793.

The Center Church has a strong commitment to intergenerational ministry, providing opportunities for people of all ages to actively participate in the life of the church.

794.

The church's archives are open to researchers and historians, allowing them to delve into the rich history of the Center Church and its impact on Hartford.

795.

The First Church of Christ has embraced technology in its worship services, incorporating multimedia presentations and live-streaming capabilities.

796.

The Center Church has been a source of inspiration for artists and writers, who have depicted its beauty and significance in various works of art and literature.

797.

The church has a strong legacy of philanthropy, supporting charitable organizations and initiatives locally and globally.

798.

The Center Church has been a voice for justice and equality, advocating for the rights of marginalized communities and promoting social change.

799.

The church's architectural features, including its towering spire and intricate detailing, are a testament to the craftsmanship of the builders.

800.

The First Church of Christ continues to be a beacon of faith, hope, and love in the Hartford community, embodying the principles of Christianity and making a positive impact on the lives of its members and the wider society.

801.

The Greater Horseshoe Bat (Rhinolophus ferrumequinum) is one of the largest bat species found in Europe.

802.

It gets its name from the horseshoe-shaped noseleaf on its face, which helps in echolocation.

803.

The Greater Horseshoe Bat has a wingspan of around 35 to 40 centimeters.

804.

It is predominantly found in Western Europe, including the United Kingdom, France, Spain, and Portugal.

805.

The species prefers roosting in caves, mines, and old buildings.

806.

Greater Horseshoe Bats are primarily insectivorous, feeding on moths, beetles, and other flying insects.

807.

They have specialized ears that allow them to detect high-frequency sounds for echolocation and prey detection.

808.

The bats emit ultrasonic calls that bounce off objects and return to them, providing information about the surroundings.

809.

Greater Horseshoe Bats are known for their slow, fluttering flight.

810.

They can fly at speeds of up to 25 kilometers per hour.

811.

These bats have a unique social structure, with maternity colonies consisting of females and their offspring.

812.

Males typically roost separately or form small bachelor groups.

813.

Greater Horseshoe Bats have a relatively long lifespan, with individuals living up to 25 years in the wild.

814.

They are highly sensitive to disturbance and can be negatively affected by human activities.

815.

The species has experienced population declines in many parts of its range due to habitat loss and degradation.

816.

Conservation efforts, including the protection of roosting sites and the creation of foraging habitats, are being undertaken to preserve the Greater Horseshoe Bat population.

817.

The bats play an important ecological role by controlling insect populations, which benefits agriculture and reduces the need for pesticides.

818.

They are considered a keystone species in their ecosystems.

819.

Greater Horseshoe Bats hibernate during the winter months, typically from November to March.

820.

Hibernation sites, known as hibernacula, are often located in caves or underground tunnels.

821.

During hibernation, the bats enter a state of torpor, lowering their body temperature and metabolic rate to conserve energy.

822.

The mating season for Greater Horseshoe Bats occurs in the autumn, with females storing the sperm until the following spring.

823.

Females give birth to a single pup each year, typically in late June or early July.

824.

The pups are born hairless and blind but quickly develop and grow.

825.

Mothers nurse their pups with milk until they are old enough to fly and feed on their own.

826.

The diet of Greater Horseshoe Bats changes throughout the year, reflecting the availability of different insect species.

827.

They are known to eat a wide variety of insects, including moths, beetles, flies, and wasps.

828.

The species has been historically associated with myths and legends, often being portrayed as symbols of darkness and mystery.

829.

Efforts to study and understand the behavior and ecology of Greater Horseshoe Bats have increased in recent years, leading to valuable insights into their conservation needs.

830.

The International Union for Conservation of Nature (IUCN) lists the Greater Horseshoe Bat as Near Threatened on the Red List of Threatened Species.

831.

The species is protected under various national and international conservation laws.

832.

Greater Horseshoe Bats have been successfully reintroduced to some areas where they had previously disappeared.

833.

They are highly susceptible to disturbances caused by artificial lighting, which can disrupt their feeding and navigation.

834.

Research has shown that the bats prefer habitats with a mosaic of different vegetation types, providing diverse foraging opportunities.

835.

The conservation of Greater Horseshoe Bats often involves the collaboration of researchers, conservation organizations, and local communities.

836.

The bats have complex vocalizations that are used for communication and mate selection.

837.

They have been observed engaging in social behaviors such as grooming and scent marking.

838.

Greater Horseshoe Bats have been studied for their unique adaptations and sensory capabilities, contributing to scientific understanding of echolocation and bat biology.

839.

The species has inspired artistic and cultural expressions, appearing in literature, artwork, and folklore.

840.

The species has inspired artistic and cultural expressions, appearing in literature, artwork, and folklore.

841.

They are recognized as important indicators of the health and biodiversity of their habitats.

842.

The bats have been the subject of research to develop innovative conservation strategies, such as creating artificial roosts and enhancing foraging habitats.

843.

Greater Horseshoe Bats have been fitted with radio transmitters to track their movements and better understand their roosting and foraging behaviors.

844.

The bats have a keen sense of hearing, which helps them locate prey in complete darkness.

845.

They have large eyes relative to their body size, allowing them to see in low-light conditions.

846.

Greater Horseshoe Bats have been found to communicate with other members of their colony using specific vocalizations.

847.

The species is known for its agility and maneuverability in flight, enabling it to navigate through complex environments.

848.

The conservation status of Greater Horseshoe Bats varies across their range, with some populations more threatened than others.

849.

Habitat restoration projects, such as the creation of wildlife-friendly landscapes, have been implemented to support the recovery of the species.

850.

Greater Horseshoe Bats are captivating creatures that continue to fascinate researchers, conservationists, and nature enthusiasts with their unique adaptations and ecological importance.

851.

The Greater Mouse-Eared Bat (Myotis myotis) is one of the largest bat species found in Europe.

852.

It gets its name from its large, mouse-like ears that are proportionally longer than those of other bat species.

853.

The species is widely distributed across Europe, from the United Kingdom to Russia and from Spain to Turkey.

854.

Greater Mouse-Eared Bats prefer roosting in caves, mines, and old buildings, often in large colonies.

855.

They are predominantly insectivorous, feeding on a variety of insects such as beetles, moths, and flies.

856.

The bats use echolocation to navigate and locate prey, emitting ultrasonic calls and interpreting the returning echoes.

857.

Greater Mouse-Eared Bats have a wingspan of about 40 to 45 centimeters.

858.

They are known for their slow, agile flight, which allows them to maneuver through cluttered environments.

859.

The bats have a distinctive appearance, with dark brown fur and a stocky body.

860.

Males and females can be distinguished by their size, with males being slightly larger.

861.

Greater Mouse-Eared Bats have a lifespan of up to 20 years in the wild.

862.

They typically form maternity colonies during the breeding season, with females giving birth to a single pup each year.

863.

The pups are born in late spring or early summer and are initially dependent on their mothers for milk.

864.

The species hibernates during the winter months, typically from November to March, in cool, humid caves.

865.

During hibernation, their body temperature drops, and their metabolism slows down to conserve energy.

866.

The bats are highly sensitive to disturbance during hibernation and may wake up if the temperature or humidity changes significantly.

867.

Greater Mouse-Eared Bats are known for their vocalizations, including social calls, mating calls, and distress calls.

868.

They are relatively sedentary bats, with a home range of about 10 to 20 kilometers.

869.

The species is listed as Near Threatened on the International Union for Conservation of Nature (IUCN) Red List.

870.

Habitat loss, disturbance, and changes in agricultural practices are the main threats to Greater Mouse-Eared Bats.

871.

Conservation efforts focus on protecting roosting sites, promoting sustainable agricultural practices, and raising awareness about the importance of bats.

872.

The bats play a crucial role in controlling insect populations, providing valuable ecosystem services.

873.

They are considered indicators of the health of their habitats, as changes in their population can reflect changes in environmental conditions.

874.

Greater Mouse-Eared Bats have been the subject of scientific research to better understand their behavior, ecology, and conservation needs.

875.

Studies have shown that the bats may forage in different habitats, including forests, grasslands, and wetlands.

876.

They have been found to use landmarks and memory to navigate between roosting sites and foraging areas.

877.

Greater Mouse-Eared Bats have been successfully reintroduced to some areas where they had become locally extinct.

878.

The bats are vulnerable to disturbances caused by human activities, such as tourism and construction near roosting sites.

879.

Climate change may also pose a threat to their habitats and foraging resources.

880.

Greater Mouse-Eared Bats have been recorded using a variety of roost types, including natural caves, artificial caves, and buildings.

881.

The bats are able to squeeze through small gaps to access their roosts, thanks to their flexible bodies.

882.

Their roosting sites provide protection from predators and a stable microclimate for rearing young and hibernating.

883.

Greater Mouse-Eared Bats have been observed engaging in social behaviors, such as grooming and vocal interactions.

884.

They are generally non-aggressive and show cooperative behaviors within their colonies.

885.

The bats are capable of flying long distances in search of suitable foraging grounds.

886.

They have been recorded flying up to 30 kilometers from their roosts to find food.

887.

Greater Mouse-Eared Bats have a preference for foraging in open habitats with abundant insect resources.

888.

They are capable of capturing prey in flight using their sharp teeth and agile flight maneuvers.

889.

The bats have been found to consume a wide variety of insects, including beetles, moths, and flies.

890.

Greater Mouse-Eared Bats have been the subject of folklore and cultural beliefs in some regions, often associated with superstitions and myths.

891.

The species has been featured in scientific literature, artwork, and conservation campaigns to raise awareness about bat conservation.

892.

Research has been conducted to investigate the acoustic characteristics of Greater Mouse-Eared Bat calls and their role in communication.

893.

The bats have been fitted with tiny radio transmitters to track their movements and study their habitat preferences.

894.

Monitoring programs have been established to assess the population trends and distribution of Greater Mouse-Eared Bats.

895.

Public education and outreach initiatives aim to dispel myths and misconceptions about bats and highlight their ecological importance.

896.

Greater Mouse-Eared Bats have been recognized as a priority species for conservation action in several European countries.

897.

Habitat management practices, such as maintaining old trees and providing artificial roosting structures, can benefit the bats.

898.

Local communities and volunteers play a vital role in monitoring and protecting Greater Mouse-Eared Bat populations.

899.

The bats are charismatic and fascinating creatures that contribute to the biodiversity and ecological balance of their habitats.

900.

Continued research, conservation efforts, and public engagement are essential for the long-term survival of Greater Mouse-Eared Bats and the ecosystems they inhabit.

901.

Canon, officially known as Canon Inc., is a Japanese multinational corporation that specializes in the manufacture of imaging and optical products, including cameras, camcorders, printers, and photocopiers.

902.

The company was founded on August 10, 1937, in Tokyo, Japan, by Takeshi Mitarai, Goro Yoshida, Saburo Uchida, and Takeo Maeda.

903.

The name "Canon" was chosen to symbolize precision and accuracy, derived from the Buddhist deity Kwanon, known for compassion and empathy.

904.

Canon's first product was the "Kwanon," a 35mm focal-plane shutter camera that was produced in prototype form but never went into mass production.

905.

The company's first commercially successful camera was the "Hansa Canon" released in 1936, featuring a unique rapid film advance mechanism.

906.

Canon entered the digital camera market in the 1980s, becoming one of the pioneers in the field of digital imaging.

907.

In 1987, Canon launched the EOS (Electro-Optical System) series of SLR cameras, which used an electronic lens mount and autofocus technology, revolutionizing the industry.

908.

Canon is known for its innovation in imaging technology, including the development of the first autofocus SLR camera, the Canon EOS 650, in 1987.

909.

The company introduced its first digital single-lens reflex (DSLR) camera, the EOS DCS 3, in 1995, marking a significant milestone in the transition from film to digital photography.

910.

Canon has a rich history of producing high-quality lenses, including the renowned L-series lenses that are favored by professional photographers for their exceptional image quality and durability.

911.

In 1992, Canon launched the EOS-1N, a professional-grade SLR camera that became widely used in the field of photojournalism and sports photography.

912.

Canon expanded its product range to include inkjet printers and multifunction devices in the late 1980s and early 1990s, establishing itself as a leading provider of printing solutions.

913.

The company introduced the "Bubble Jet" technology in 1985, which allowed for high-quality color printing with inkjet printers.

914.

Canon has a strong presence in the business and professional printing industry, offering a wide range of commercial printers, production printers, and large-format printers.

915.

In 2000, Canon launched the Canon EOS-1D, the company's flagship digital SLR camera designed for professional photographers.

916.

Canon has made significant contributions to the medical imaging field, producing a wide range of medical devices, including X-ray systems, ultrasound machines, and ophthalmic equipment.

917.

The company has also been involved in the development of cutting-edge technologies such as 3D printing, augmented reality (AR), and virtual reality (VR).

918.

Canon has a strong commitment to environmental sustainability and has implemented various initiatives to reduce its environmental impact, including energy-efficient products and recycling programs.

919.

The company has received numerous awards and accolades for its products and innovations, including several prestigious Technical Image Press Association (TIPA) awards.

920.

Canon is actively involved in corporate social responsibility (CSR) initiatives, supporting various charitable causes, educational programs, and environmental conservation efforts.

921.

The Canon Foundation was established in 2008 to provide financial support for scientific research and cultural exchange activities.

922.

Canon's products are sold worldwide, and the company has a strong global presence with subsidiaries and manufacturing facilities in various countries.

923.

Canon's logo, known as the "Kwanon Mark," features an image of the Buddhist deity Kwanon holding a camera lens.

924.

The company's headquarters, known as the Canon Tokyo Building, is located in Tokyo's Ota City.

925.

Canon has a long-standing partnership with the Olympic Games, serving as an official sponsor and providing imaging equipment for capturing iconic moments during the Games.

926.

Canon has a dedicated research and development (R&D) division focused on advancing imaging technology and exploring new possibilities in the field of optics.

927.

The company has filed numerous patents for its inventions and continues to invest heavily in R&D to stay at the forefront of imaging innovation.

928.

Canon is listed on the Tokyo Stock Exchange and has consistently been ranked among the top companies in Japan in terms of market capitalization.

929.

The company has a strong emphasis on quality control and is known for its stringent manufacturing standards, ensuring reliable and durable products.

930.

Canon's products are widely used by professionals in various industries, including photography, filmmaking, broadcasting, and graphic arts.

931.

Canon has a diverse product portfolio, ranging from entry-level consumer cameras to high-end professional cinema cameras, catering to the needs of different user segments.

932.

The company has established a reputation for its user-friendly interfaces and intuitive camera controls, making its products accessible to photographers of all skill levels.

933.

Canon has a strong presence in the video production industry, offering a range of professional cinema cameras and lenses used in filmmaking and television production.

934.

Canon has been at the forefront of technological advancements in the imaging industry, including the development of high-resolution image sensors and image stabilization technologies.

935.

The company has a dedicated line of compact cameras, known as the PowerShot series, offering versatile features and advanced imaging capabilities in a portable form factor.

936.

Canon has a robust system of customer support, offering technical assistance, firmware updates, and educational resources to help users maximize their product experience.

937.

The company has a strong online presence, with an official website that provides comprehensive product information, tutorials, and a platform for customer engagement.

938.

Canon has a significant presence in the professional printing market, supplying printers and presses for commercial printing, photo labs, and graphic arts applications.

939.

The company has established strategic partnerships and collaborations with other industry leaders, fostering innovation and expanding its product offerings.

940.

Canon has a strong commitment to diversity and inclusion, promoting equal opportunities and fostering a supportive work environment.

941.

The company's employees are known as "Canonites" and are encouraged to embrace a culture of creativity, collaboration, and continuous learning.

942.

Canon has a strong brand reputation for producing reliable, high-quality products that are trusted by professionals and consumers alike.

943.

The company has been recognized for its ethical business practices and has been included in various sustainability and corporate responsibility indices.

944.

Canon's commitment to social responsibility extends to its supply chain, with policies in place to ensure responsible sourcing and fair labor practices.

945.

The company has a dedicated program called "Canon for Education" that aims to support educational institutions with technology and resources.

946.

Canon actively participates in industry trade shows, exhibitions, and photography events, showcasing its latest products and engaging with customers and enthusiasts.

947.

The company has a robust marketing and advertising strategy, featuring prominent photographers and filmmakers to showcase the capabilities of its products.

948.

Canon has a strong presence in the professional sports photography field, with its cameras and lenses widely used by sports photographers to capture action-packed moments.

949.

The company has a strong commitment to innovation and regularly introduces new products and technologies to meet the evolving needs of the imaging industry.

950.

Canon's legacy in the imaging industry is marked by its contributions to photography and visual storytelling, empowering individuals to capture and share their creative vision.

951.

Western Digital Corporation, commonly known as WD, is an American computer hard disk drive manufacturer and data storage company.

952.

The company was founded on April 23, 1970, by Alvin B. Phillips, Jr., and was originally named General Digital.

953.

Western Digital's first product was the WD1402A UART (Universal Asynchronous Receiver-Transmitter) chip, which became popular in the early days of personal computing.

954.

In 1975, Western Digital introduced its first hard disk drive, the WD1405A, with a capacity of 14 megabytes.

955.

Western Digital played a significant role in the development of the ATA (Advanced Technology Attachment) interface, which became the standard interface for connecting hard drives to computers.

956.

In 1988, Western Digital introduced the Caviar series of hard drives, which offered higher capacities and faster data transfer rates.

957.

Western Digital expanded its product portfolio to include external hard drives, solid-state drives (SSDs), and network-attached storage (NAS) solutions.

958.

In 1997, Western Digital acquired the hard drive business of IBM, significantly expanding its market share and product offerings.

959.

The company introduced its first consumer-focused external hard drive, the WD Personal Storage, in 2000, targeting home users and small businesses.

960.

Western Digital acquired the storage systems division of Silicon Graphics (SGI) in 2001, further strengthening its position in the enterprise storage market.

961.

In 2006, Western Digital introduced the first 2.5-inch SATA hard drive with a capacity of 500 gigabytes, offering high storage density in a compact form factor.

962.

Western Digital entered the solid-state drive market in 2009 with the introduction of the SiliconDrive line of SSDs.

963.

In 2012, Western Digital acquired Hitachi Global Storage Technologies, becoming one of the largest manufacturers of hard drives in the world.

964.

Western Digital introduced its first helium-filled hard drives, the HGST Ultrastar He6 series, in 2013, offering higher capacities and improved energy efficiency.

965.

The company launched the WD Red series of NAS hard drives in 2012, specifically designed for home and small office network storage systems.

966.

Western Digital expanded its presence in the flash storage market with the acquisition of SanDisk Corporation in 2016, becoming a leading manufacturer of SSDs and flash memory products.

967.

In 2017, Western Digital unveiled the world's first 14-terabyte hard drive, offering exceptional storage capacity for enterprise applications.

968.

The company introduced the WD Black line of gaming hard drives in 2019, offering high-performance storage solutions for gamers and enthusiasts.

969.

Western Digital has been actively involved in research and development in the field of data storage, exploring technologies such as heat-assisted magnetic recording (HAMR) and microwave-assisted magnetic recording (MAMR) for future hard drives.

970.

Western Digital has a strong presence in the surveillance industry, offering specialized hard drives and storage solutions for video surveillance systems.

971.

The company's products are used in various industries, including automotive, aerospace, healthcare, and entertainment, where reliable and high-capacity storage is essential.

972.

Western Digital has manufacturing facilities and research centers located worldwide, including in the United States, Thailand, Malaysia, and China.

973.

The company has received numerous awards and accolades for its products, including recognition for its innovation in storage technology and design.

974.

Western Digital is committed to environmental sustainability and has implemented various initiatives to reduce energy consumption and promote responsible waste management.

975.

The company actively participates in community outreach programs and charitable initiatives, supporting education, disaster relief efforts, and environmental conservation.

976.

Western Digital is listed on the NASDAQ stock exchange under the ticker symbol "WDC" and is a constituent of the S&P 500 index.

977.

The company has a strong focus on data security, offering features such as hardware encryption and data recovery services to protect and safeguard customer data.

978.

Western Digital has a customer support network that provides technical assistance, warranty services, and software updates to ensure optimal performance of its products.

979.

The company has a strong commitment to quality control and adheres to strict manufacturing standards to deliver reliable and durable storage solutions.

980.

Western Digital is actively involved in standards organizations and industry consortiums to drive the development of new storage technologies and promote interoperability.

981.

The company has a diverse workforce, with employees from different backgrounds and cultures contributing to its global operations.

982.

Western Digital is a member of the Storage Networking Industry Association (SNIA), an industry group that promotes standards and best practices in storage networking.

983.

The company's products undergo rigorous testing and certification processes to ensure compatibility with a wide range of devices and platforms.

984.

Western Digital has a strong research and development focus, investing in cutting-edge technologies to stay at the forefront of the data storage industry.

985.

The company has a strong brand reputation for its reliability, performance, and innovation in the storage market.

986.

Western Digital has been recognized for its corporate social responsibility efforts, including its commitment to ethical business practices and social impact initiatives.

987.

The company has a strong online presence, providing comprehensive product information, support resources, and a platform for customer engagement.

988.

Western Digital actively engages with its customer community through online forums, user groups, and social media platforms to gather feedback and improve its products and services.

989.

The company's products are sold worldwide through various channels, including retailers, distributors, and online marketplaces.

990.

Western Digital has a strong commitment to continuous improvement and invests in research and development to address evolving customer needs and industry trends.

991.

The company has a strong intellectual property portfolio, with numerous patents related to storage technologies and innovations.

992.

Western Digital has a proactive approach to data privacy and security, complying with industry regulations and implementing measures to protect customer data.

993.

The company actively collaborates with technology partners, software vendors, and system integrators to deliver comprehensive storage solutions for various applications.

994.

Western Digital has a dedicated team focused on data analytics and data management, helping customers optimize their storage infrastructure and extract value from their data.

995.

The company has a track record of successful partnerships and joint ventures to expand its product offerings and address emerging market trends.

996.

Western Digital supports open-source initiatives and contributes to the development of open standards in the storage industry.

997.

The company's leadership team comprises experienced professionals with diverse expertise in technology, engineering, and business management.

998.

Western Digital fosters a culture of innovation and encourages its employees to explore new ideas and push the boundaries of technology.

999.

The company actively monitors industry trends and consumer preferences to anticipate future demands and develop products that meet evolving market needs.

1000.

Western Digital's history and success in the data storage industry have positioned it as a trusted partner for individuals, businesses, and organizations seeking reliable and scalable storage solutions.